Do you want to sell more copies of your self-published book? Of course you do. This book reveals *how* you will achieve publishing success.

Discover which sales and marketing tactics are generating results for other authors. Learn how the modern book publishing industry actually functions, including little-known practices that could hold the key to your profitability. Each concept is explained and illustrated with inspiring true-life stories of authors who have achieved success on their own terms.

In this book, Bruce Batchelor – who invented the print-on-demand publishing process that has enabled independent authors to sell tens of millions of books – helps you pick *which specific marketing efforts will be most time-efficient and cost-effective for you, your book and your purpose.*

By creating the right marketing mix, you will be successful in selling your book *and* will enjoy yourself along the way!

Book
Marketing
DeMystified:
SELF-PUBLISHING
SUCCESS

BRUCE T. BATCHELOR

Hey Jordan —
Thanks for creating,
networking, encouraging —
cheers, Bruce February 2011

Agio
PUBLISHING HOUSE

PUBLISHING HOUSE

151 Howe Street, Victoria BC Canada V8V 4K5

For information and bulk orders, please contact:
info@agiopublishing.com *or go to* www.agiopublishing.com

Book Marketing DeMystified: Self-Publishing Success
[first released in 2007; updated in 2010]
ISBN   978-1-897435-00-7 (trade paperback - English language)
       987-1-897435-02-1 (electronic edition - English)
       978-1-897435-04-5 (trade paperback - German)

Printed on acid-free paper. Agio Publishing House is a socially
responsible company, measuring success on a triple-bottom-line
basis.

To contact the author, go to www.agiopublishing.com
or visit his blog at www.bookmarketing.agiopublishing.com

10   9   8   7   6   5   4   3   2 - b

DEDICATED

to all the indie authors who shared their stories,
my thanks to each of you,

and to Marsha, Dan and Tyhee!

TABLE OF CONTENTS

About the author and
my perspective on selling and marketing books

Probably just like you, I've had a lifelong love of books. From following along as my mother read to me as a toddler, through my pre-teen years captivated by the *Biggles* and *Hardy Boys* books, I was mightily impressed with the printed word. Then, while working on my high school's yearbook, I discovered that one could *create* books simply by being so bold as to typeset the words and pay a printer to make bound copies! After that, there was no stopping me.

In the 1970s, I wrote, self-published and successfully marketed two bestselling books, doing so independently – without the help of a conventional publishing house – somewhat oblivious to how selling books was supposed to be so terribly difficult. The marketing for those two titles was so obvious and straightforward that I thought the selling and marketing for *all* books would be as simple. I no longer believe that!

For the past 30 years, I've worked at editing, ghost-writing, publishing and marketing, sometimes with conventional publishing houses and more often assisting the self-publishing authors who bravely live on the fringes of the book industry.

During these three decades, my wife Marsha and I also operated a communications consultancy. We created marketing programs for business, non-profit and government clients. We designed and typeset literally thousands of books, magazine issues, brochures, technical manuals, reports, newsletters and ad campaigns. Generally, I was involved in the writing and editing of each job to some extent and Marsha was the graphic designer. We won numerous awards; the most gratifying ones were for the *effectiveness* of campaigns, rather than prettiness. I've taught Marketing at the college level, and also worked as a newspaper journalist and magazine editor. When writing assignments scarce I worked as a surveyor, fisherman and parks patrolman. Going way back, I was a computer programmer, and earned an honors degree in pure mathematics. Immediately after university, I lived in a geodesic dome log cabin in the Yukon, sometimes going on long winter camping trips with a team of sled dogs, and often just sitting and thinking.

That eclectic background provided me with a unique perspective in 1994 to foresee an amazing opportunity emerging from the convergence of certain technologies and trends. Print-on-Demand (POD) equipment + the Internet 'information super-highway' + Internet search engines + credit cards + e-commerce + desktop publishing + email + Adobe Post-Script™ + authors anxious to be published.... I envisioned a book publishing service that would help independent ('indie') authors everywhere. It would conduct most of its business over the new Internet, and would use print-on-demand manufacturing to produce only as many books as needed. To keep costs to the absolute minimum, we would go one step beyond 'just-in-time' inventory to be totally 'on-demand,' printing the books only *after* an order came in. If only one copy was ordered, we only printed ONE copy. Most people thought I was nuts.

Within a year, Trafford Publishing had been formed and we had our first paying clients. These were pioneering authors who were departing from the book industry's old distribution model (of having preprinted books sitting in warehouses and on bookstore shelves on a consignment basis), for the untested concept of promoting and selling books largely over the Internet.

Happily, by 1996, Amazon.com had begun to popularize the concept of buying books over the Internet. As well, Baker & Taylor, one of the USA's largest book distributors, had set up POD equipment to print back-list titles for publishing houses, calling their service Replica Books. Then Ingram Book, the world's largest book distributor, built a monster POD printing factory in Tennessee beside their largest warehouse, so that POD books could flow into Ingram's distribution system and out to bookstores and online retailers with all the other books. Initially called Lightning Print, this print service later became Lightning Source Inc. [LSI]. Soon other companies opened and adopted Trafford's POD business model of serving independent authors: Xlibris, iUniverse, AuthorHouse, Infinity, BookLocker, Outskirts, Spire, Xulon and dozens of others. Now some newer publishing services, such as Lulu.com and Blurb.com, offer on-demand book printing without book trade distribution. More recently, Amazon opened its own publishing service, called CreateSpace. It seems the whole world has discovered print-on-demand publishing.

During my 11 years as Trafford's founding publisher and CEO, it grew to become one of the world's most prolific publishing houses with more than 10,000 active titles from indie authors living in more than 100 countries. Currently, thanks to all the POD publishing services combined, about 200,000 new authors are published *every year*!

We authors are now entering a wonderful new chapter in indie publishing, highlighted by ever-expanding distribution using eBook editions, audio books and truly global POD production, and great online promotional opportunities.

Helping authors realize their dreams is magical for me. In 2006, I left my leadership position at Trafford to return to working personally with authors, their manuscripts and those dreams. [Trafford was later acquired by competitor Author Solutions Inc.] Once again, as we did before launching the POD revolution, my wife and I are operating a small publishing company – *Agio Publishing House*. We are pioneering a new form of publishing service, based on a collaborative decision-making and financing model, and highest quality writing, editing and design. I feel very fortunate and privileged to be editing and advising creative people.

Marketing a book has parallels to the marketing of any other product or service. With that reality in mind, I've organized all the explanations and interviews in this book using a 14-P framework that can be used for conceptualizing and planning *any* marketing effort. Each chapter discusses an aspect of marketing that begins with the letter P. So you'll be reading about purpose, price, place, partnerships... and so on.

The book trade has many characteristics (some are rather bizarre and counter-intuitive) that are distinct from other retail sectors, so each chapter begins with some describing of the business situations you'll encounter. The majority of my book marketing experience is North American, so if you are an author from another continent, it may take you a bit of research to discover regional business differences and opportunities. For example, I'm told book launches are more lucrative – and definitely more fun – in Ireland than in urban North America!

A big thank you to all the authors who graciously told me about their experiences, and whose stories appear in the chapters.

I do hope you enjoy *Book Marketing DeMystified: Self-Publishing Success*, finding it both educational and motivating. You can read my latest commentaries about publishing at my blog: www.bookmarketing. agiopublishing.com. Please email me (info@agiopublishing.com) your marketing stories and suggestions for updates to this book.

Thanks, cheers!
Bruce Batchelor

The marketing mix framework – your template for conceptualizing and planning

The sales and marketing advice presented in this book will give you a huge boost, whether you have a contract with a mainstream publisher, or are an independent ('indie') author publishing all on your own or with the assistance of a publishing service.

Book publishing can be defined as *causing a book to be in a printed form and available to the public for purchase*. Over the past decade, the first part – getting *a book into printed form* – has been dramatically simplified and is much less expensive due to Print-on-Demand (POD) manufacturing. POD allows publishers and authors to avoid paying for a large print run and managing an inventory, yet to still have exactly as many printed books as needed. Pages of a POD book can be in full color or black on white; the binding can be paperback or casebound (hardback) with either a dust jacket or a laminated cover.

The second part of the definition – making books *available to the public for purchase* – has been a responsibility traditionally shared by the publisher and the author. *Making available* can be thought of as having two components: making potential buyers *aware* of your book, and ensuring copies are readily *accessible* for those buyers to purchase.

Depending on your publishing house or service, you will have access to different tools for building the awareness and accessibility. This guide will help you, as a new author, better understand the bookselling environment so you can be most effective with your marketing initiatives – at whatever scale and by whatever means you decide to promote your book. Better understanding means a better plan, which will bring you self-publishing success!

MARKETING IS NOT THE SAME AS HIGH-PRESSURE SELLING

Some people are paralyzed by the irrational notion that *marketing* is synonymous with personally badgering people, somehow coercing them into buying something they don't particularly want or need. Relax! You really don't need to transform yourself into an obsessive, self-promoting ego-maniac to be successful.

Such common misconceptions can prevent an author from seeing that marketing is actually a creative exercise, an intriguing puzzle-solving process with limitless possibilities. Authors are very creative people and, therefore, well-equipped to find marvelous solutions. All they need is a practical framework for decision-making, plus some basic knowledge of the book trade and the available options.

For the sales and marketing of your book to be sustainable, one needs to find a balance – weighing one's home, work and other priorities on one hand, with your time and financial commitment to book selling on the other. Balance is easiest to sustain if you can select tactics that suit your fancy, so you can *enjoy* promoting your book, rather than feeling drained or uncomfortable. This book presents many options to consider and true stories of other authors' experiences. I've confidence you can find the time and make the commitment to carry out a few high-payoff promotional activities. After all, you had the personal discipline to write an entire book, didn't you?

This guide is to help you identify marketing strategies that match your purpose and resources. I will:

- provide a practical framework for planning your sales and marketing efforts,
- explain the often bizarre workings of the book industry, and
- give practical examples that have proven to be effective and fun for other authors.

Before you and I go any further, let's agree on what 'marketing' means and entails.

Surprisingly, even though one can get an advanced university degree in Marketing, there is no consensus in academia nor in the business world about a precise definition of the word *marketing*. I know this because I have taught Marketing at the college level! Imagine the confusion when I moved on to manage a communications consultancy, and clients would say marketing when they meant some, but not all, of: in-person selling, or advertising, or setting up distribution networks, or promoting franchises or running contests or just about anything. This was frustrating, at times embarrassing, and counter-productive – until I devised the definition shown below. This definition is the conceptual framework for the marketing mix you will develop while reading this book. This framework has been used with remarkable success to build tens of millions of dollars of wealth for authors and other business clients.

When you are developing a marketing strategy in any line of business, you are thinking about how to allocate resources and align your efforts in a number of areas simultaneously, trying to juggle priorities. The classical 'marketing mix' asserts there are only four aspects (the '4-Ps') to be considered: product, price, place and promotions. This definition of the marketing mix was created by Jerome McCarthy in his 1960 book called *Basic Marketing: A Managerial Approach*. In the real world, the

4-P framework is clearly inadequate. I propose that you use the following more robust definition with 14-Ps when you are plotting how to sell your new book.

Marketing is the process of **creating, implementing, monitoring and updating a strategy** for the complete **marketing mix**, which is:

    having a needed **product** (or service)

    available at a convenient **place** (and time)

    for a mutually satisfactory **price** (value),

    while ensuring that the correct segments of the **public**

    are aware (the **promotional mix**)

    and motivated (**positioning**),

    all in a manner which takes advantage of strategic **partnerships**

    and contributes to the overall **purpose** (passion).

The **promotional mix** includes

    personal sales,

    publicity & public relations,

    paid advertising,

    and sales **promotions**.

Ideally, this will be done with respect and consideration to the 'triple-bottom-line' of

    financial **profits**,

    the **planet** (our environment)

    and **people** (society).

While you digest that mouthful of Ps, consider that, as you solve your book's marketing mix puzzle, you'll often be substituting creativity and personal connections for the brute-force, expensive strategies employed by the large publishing houses. Here's a rather blunt assessment of conventional book marketing by Richard Balkin:

Of all the major industries in the United States, surely book publishing is the most primitive, the most disorganized, and the most haphazard. Consider the following: What other industry would launch a national campaign for an untested product whose life span is usually less than a year and whose chances of recouping its investment are worse than one in three? What other industry would manufacture so many competing products with only the barest notion of which of them might succeed in the market-place? What other industry would sink a hefty percentage of its capital into a variety of mechanisms designed to stimulate sales, knowing full well that the most effective method – that elusive 'word of mouth' – is totally beyond its control? In many ways, a publisher acts like a Hopi shaman praying for rain: They both execute a number of rituals designed to convince themselves and their followers that they can control uncontrollable events, and then go home and cross their fingers. If rain doesn't fall, they blame themselves or their acolytes for not adequately perform-ing some of the rituals, thereby angering the gods and spoiling the magic. 'Go out and get some really smooth stones this time,' they say, 'and let's try again.' [from Richard Balkin, *A Writer's Guide to Book Publishing*, pp 199–200, Plume Publishers, 1994, ISBN 0452270219]

That sounds pretty gloomy and Richard didn't even touch on the financially-suicidal practice of selling books on 'returnable' terms. But, hey, don't get too discouraged by Richard's assessment. He was writing about the conventional book industry, not what indie authors are now ac-complishing. [His book does have excellent information about the tradi-tional industry.] Remember: with a little knowledge and clever choices in your 14-P marketing mix, you can be way more cost-effective at selling your book than the industry pros. You'll create a world of possibilities so you won't need those really smooth stones.

Why did you write your book? The answer is *very* important – as you will see, we'll keep coming back throughout this book to your motivation (your **purpose** or **passion**).

Each author's reasons for writing are unique. Some want to change the behavior of others (possibly by teaching the reader about health or religion or politics). The simple desire to entertain is the motivating force for some writers, while many others feel compelled to record memories of a time and place they cherish. A book can be an essential tool to build a consulting or public speaking career. It could be the proud unveiling of a lifelong compulsion to create poetry or invent a sci-fi series. Some people use the independent (self-) publishing process as a market test, hoping to attract the attention of a film producer or impress the acquisitions editor at a major publishing house. Your motives may have the long-term time frame of introducing a romance trilogy or series of thrillers one at a time – or could have more urgency. A few writers blatantly proclaim their quest for fame and fortune, while others value their privacy and time too much to thrust themselves 100% into promotional efforts. All are valid reasons, none better than others.

Before you read the next chapters, please take a moment to write out a few sentences about your purpose. It need not be eloquent.

PLANNING THE MARKETING MIX

At its most basic, your marketing plan can be as simple as answering the questions at the start of each chapter *(the questions are also found in the marketing mix template on page 159)*. If you answer these questions, you'll be way ahead of most other self-promoting authors and many industry pros because you'll have a clear overview and can focus on those factors you've decided to emphasize. As important, you'll have decided, and are comfortable with the decision, on what *not* to do.

As mentioned previously, this guide is organized into chapters, one for each of these 14-P factors. We'll describe the business situation and provide examples of what other authors have done. As we go along, you can be thinking about your book and jotting down ideas for your marketing plan.

Ready? *Allons-y!* Here's a delicious story to illustrate how to concoct a great marketing mix.

THE GREAT TASTE OF SELF-PUBLISHING SUCCESS!

Back in 1981, Joan Bidinosti and Marilyn Wearring, two women living in rural Ontario, decided to create and market: "the best book we could. We did a lot of research and really thought things out," Joan told me. "We wanted to make a book that *we* liked. We wanted to be proud of it, then hoped other people would like it. Making money really didn't enter into it."

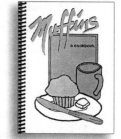

They ignored conventional wisdom in the publishing trade and created a book on a single theme: muffins. *Muffins: A Cookbook* [ISBN 0969134509] didn't have photographs (supposedly another nono), nor a hard cover. Instead they created a quite small, handy, coil-bound book. They tested every recipe thoroughly, had only one recipe per page and the page number clearly visible in large type. Directions were numbered and simply explained. The oven temperature and baking time were at the top.

Baking tips were printed on a colored sheet of paper inserted at the book's center – this helped cooks navigate by remembering if a favorite recipe was before or after the middle. Joan's daughter, Susan, created whimsical drawings for the cover and insides.

They knew the ideal gift price: $4.95 (this was back in 1981), and found a printer who could work within their budget. One thousand copies were printed, a few letters sent to the local media, and the two authors took the first copies to a gift store and a book store. At the curling rink and exercise class, Marilyn sold copies to her friends who came back to buy more copies for their friends. Within a week, the local TV news program ran a short item, which prompted the newspaper to run a full-page story.

From that point on, the two authors had a tiger by the tail. During the next decade, they sold over 200,000 copies of *Muffins: A Cookbook*, plus 60,000 copies of a sequel called *Salads: A Cookbook*.

Looking back, Joan can reminisce about dozens of successful marketing initiatives. The authors made hundreds of **personal sales** appearances in department stores, bookstores, gift shops, trade shows... always passing out delicious samples and always selling large quantities of books.

There was a sheet on the last page of the book, providing an address for ordering more copies, with a discount for ordering 5 or more. "It was word-of-mouth through friends who liked everything about it that sold our book," Joan believes. "We'd get lovely letters with the mail orders."

What was Joan and Marilyn's marketing mix? They had a clear **purpose** which led them to create – often at odds with expert advice – a remarkably useful and likeable **product** at an ideal **price** point. With that solid foundation, any and all **promotions** worked well.

"Luck follows hard work," says Joan about the research they did in advance.

By careful attention to the **purpose**, **product** and **price** factors in their marketing mix, these authors had a winning recipe, and achieved spectacular results. We'll tell you more about other clever sales techniques used for *Muffins: A Cookbook* in later chapters.

Read on to learn how others have found marketing mix solutions, so you too can mix those Ps, solve the puzzle and achieve self-publishing success!

CHAPTER 1

Purpose/passion

What is your overall goal or purpose?

How will you define and measure success?

Can you spell out the goal or goals in terms of personal aspirations, profit, mission or mandate?

What do you stand to gain? How will your life change if you are successful?

What will you lose by failure to achieve your goal(s)?

Each author's reasons for writing are unique. Please take a moment to be introspective and to list your key motivations, and you can then decide which are the top priorities.

Why should you write down an honest statement of your purpose? Because knowing 'why' will guide your decisions in the rest of the marketing mix.

Here's an example. In 1994, Fred and Peg Francis wrote *Democratic Rules of Order: The Complete Official Parliamentary Authority for*

Meetings of Any Size [ISBN 096992604] not to make money but to have a beneficial impact on society.

Democratic Rules of Order is the one parliamentary standard that fully protects every member's right to equal participation in orderly meetings. It does this with concise, common sense rules without jargon or unnecessary protocol.

Fred wrote this on their website at www.democratic-rules.com: "This book has been a very satisfying project for Fred and Peg who see the urgent need for more justice and stronger democracies in our world. For a democracy to work successfully the populace itself must understand and want to obey the democratic principles. Citizens need practice in making the individual rights of each member and the rights of the majority work together. People using this book are practicing and learning these laws at the grass-roots level."

This very concise book (27 pages of rules, a 14-page sample meeting plus questions-and-answers) explains meeting rules that are fair and easy for everyone to master – a far cry from the 600-plus pages of *Robert's Rules of Order*! With *Roberts*, a knowledgeable chair can manipulate meetings to have his or her own opinion prevail. With *Democratic*, everyone knows the rules and is on equal footing.

For Fred and Peg, a marketing plan had to reflect their mission, so they hired an editor to polish the text, making the book as understandable and credible as possible. They felt that this was really worthwhile, even though editing cost $30 per hour.

Next, they decided to start a word-of-mouth phenomenon by donating about 2,000 promotional copies to leaders of church groups, associations of government agencies, schools and public libraries. This helped them secure free book reviews in religious newsletters and in magazines that go out to politicians, bureaucrats and educators. The front pages of the book explain clearly how to order more copies, and the generous discounts for ordering larger quantities.

Fred was a mathematician who could master their marketing mix puzzle about allocating scarce resources: they refined their **product** by using a professional editor over many editions, sent out samples (a form of **sales promotion**) to targeted groups (their **public**), allowed bulk discounts (**pricing**), and sought **publicity** through newsletter and magazine reviews.

Fred and Peg's plan has worked very well – the book is now in its 7th edition and has sold over 14,000 copies, sometimes purchased in batches of over a hundred by a single congregation or agency. Copies are being used in some high schools to teach parliamentary procedures in social studies courses. Buyers often reorder and refer others to this handy book, creating a chain reaction that is steadily spreading to people all around the world who are now able to have more effective meetings.

If your purpose is to help a particular group of people, that fact will provide focus for your plans. Karen Couture did extensive research before and after she underwent a double-lung transplantation operation. She then wrote *The Lung Transplantation Handbook: A Guide for Patients* [ISBN 1552125041] to share her encyclopedic knowledge with others who would be receiving transplants, their families and the caregivers. Since sharing knowledge was her prime purpose (not 'making money' or 'becoming famous by being on Oprah'), Karen chose to link up with transplant recipients groups, such as Second Wind (www.2ndwind.org), to publicize the  book to all hospitals and specialists who perform the operation. Proceeds from sales go in part to the groups. The result? *The Lung Transplantation Handbook* is the world's top selling book on that subject, and is widely considered a 'must-have' for all prospective lung transplant recipients and their families.

Karen Couture's book has also encouraged the publishing of other books for that niche audience, including *Taking Flight: Inspirational*

Stories of Lung Transplantation, complied by Joanne M. Schum [ISBN 1553696840] and *I Call My New Lung Tina: Inspiration from a Transplant Survivor*, by Shirley Jewett [ISBN 1553952707].

Considering Karen's **purpose** of educating people, her marketing has been a fantastic success. Her goal pointed directly to the optimal marketing strategy: enlisting the active support of transplant recipient groups and their networks around the world (a **partnership**). In effect, she recruited a huge team working on **personal sales** to reach prospective transplant recipients, family and caregivers (her targeted **public**).

Chris Lear, a competitive cross country runner and freelance sportswriter, knew all about focusing on one's personal goals. Chris saw publishing through an on-demand service as a cost-effective and fast way to refine and market-test his new book in order to get 'scouted' up to the  major leagues of publishing. Chris threw himself full-time into publicity and promotion: speaking at athletic meets and camps, ensuring that elite running stores were displaying the book, securing reviews from *Sports Illustrated*, *USA Today* and other media, contacting everyone he knew. Meanwhile early readers were providing comments that fed into 30(!) rounds of revisions and corrections to perfect his story. The book was *Running With The Buffaloes: A Season Inside with Mark Wetmore, Adam Goucher and the University of Colorado's Men's Cross Country Team.*

The result of Chris's 6-month marketing sprint? Chris's book was high on Amazon.com's sports bestseller list, and The Lyons Press offered him a contract – with an impressive advance on royalties – for a new hardcover edition [ISBN 9781585743285] with a national advertising and publicity budget. Chris had won his first race as an author and was soon commissioned to write another running classic called *Sub 4:00: Alan Webb and the Quest for the Fastest Mile* [Rodale Books, ISBN 9781579547462].

Chris's **purpose** (getting his book picked up by a major sports publishing house) pointed to the optimal marketing mix solution: refining his **product** while promoting through **publicity** and **personal sales**, and ensuring it was available in influential **place**s.

Many authors want to have an impact on others' behavior or health. Acknowledging that purpose will help you ignore the distractions and plot a course that works.

What's your purpose? Maybe it is:

- educating
- entertaining
- building a career (possibly as a writer)
- recording history
- learning about publishing
- earning money
- getting critical opinions on your writing
- finding a soul mate
- fame.

A 'hidden agenda' was delightfully realized by an author from Indiana in 2002. As Harry was writing his book of fishing tales, he kept wondering what a particular girl from his high school class would think, almost four decades later, of his talents and new status as a published author. He returned to his hometown for a book signing – and she was there in the line-up! They chatted briefly as he autographed her copy, agreeing to meet for coffee afterward.

Within a year they were married! Recognizing that his underlying **purpose** was sparking a romance with that high school sweetie, we can see that Harry's choice to **publicize** (through having a book signing) at the right **place** (his hometown) was the perfect solution to his marketing mix puzzle.

How does one top a love story like that? Well, if age counts, we need to think about an octogenarian from Wisconsin. Russell is old enough to be Harry's father, but he too found himself pining for his high school belle. The novel he wrote about a young man pursuing the most beautiful girl in all the land – or at least in all the neighborhood – was cited by a reviewer as "Moving, wistful, romantic, yet with a single ray of future hope... a most memorable and engaging story."

Russell never did connect with the long-lost girlfriend. She'd moved away; maybe she had since died, who knows? However, one day a woman contacted him to say that she'd absolutely loved the novel, certain that it was the most romantic story she'd ever read. Could she possibly meet the author?

Six months later they married in Las Vegas. And have lived happily ever after.

Even if your purpose isn't as clear as that of Fred, Chris, Karen or Harry, and may have multiple components, it is very important to write out what you hope to accomplish before you get bombarded with advice and caught up in various promotions. Maybe your purpose can be to learn about publishing and book marketing, and to have fun every step of the way.

CHAPTER 2

Product or service

What product or service will you provide?

What are the tangible results for someone buying and using your product – what do the 'deliverables' look like?

What product development and market research are you doing (such as examining competing products)?

Many authors will initially think what they are selling is simply 'a book' until they pause and consider that most of us don't buy 'books' – instead we are actually buying entertainment, or advice and hope for becoming thinner/sexier/richer/smarter, or inspiration to find happiness and fulfillment, or a gift for a relative, or how-to information on parenting or investing, etc., etc.

Georgina Cronin was under no illusion that she'd be selling mere words on paper when she began writing *Size Matters – Especially When You Weigh 330 lbs* [ISBN 1553955595], her weight-loss story and how-to manual. From her base in rural Ireland, she'd successfully counseled hundreds of overweight people and knew that they needed *hope* and

15

inspiration, and a program to see them through the life-long process of gaining control over one's eating patterns.

Georgina's understanding of her **product** led to a **publicity** campaign beginning with mass-circulation Irish and English newspapers. She would appear at the editorial offices, showing 'before' photos and offering herself as dramatic proof of her program's effectiveness. She'd lost 11 stone (156 lbs.) and has kept that weight off for over 6 years. The newspapers ran full-page features on this inspiring story.

Before and after full-length photos of Georgina are used on the book's covers and all publicity materials. Clearly the purchasers would be connecting on an emotional level, hoping to try the program themselves or to give the book to a friend or relative who needed inspiration.

Georgina took so much enjoyment in having a book in print, and in publicizing her book and weight-loss program, that she and husband David have set up a book publishing and marketing service called Moyhill Publishing (www.moyhill.com) at their new home in Spain. She continues to counsel about healthy eating. Now Georgina is providing *hope* and *inspiration* to both the overweight and aspiring authors.

Martha Knight Foster wrote a humorous and heartwarming account of her mid-life crises in her novel *I Never Woke Up 'Til I Was Forty* [ISBN 1553954408]. She sent a draft copy to the famous comedienne Phyllis Diller with a letter telling Diller how she was an inspiration for Martha's writing style. Diller wrote Martha back to thank her and gave her book this glowing endorsement: "It is fabulous funny reading. LOVE, Phyllis Diller."

By including Diller's comments on the book's back cover and all marketing materials, suddenly Martha had transformed her **product** from 'just any novel' – into a *'fabulous funny reading' experience* endorsed by one of America's top celebrities.

When Jill Tomlin of Cobh, County Cork, Ireland, wrote a children's story, she didn't stop there. She wanted to create a lasting contribution to the local cultural heritage that would captivate youngsters and be embraced by people throughout the region. So Jill commissioned a local girl to illustrate her story and hired another girl to recite the words for a CD that would be included. What started as a simple story was now a colorful picture book and audio recording package.

The party to launch Jill's self-published *The Famous Seamus* [ISBN 1412015111] was a merry event, with hundreds of townsfolk present, including the mayor and council, clergy, educators and other notables. Everyone listened in awe to the recital, the girls were toasted, and politicians proclaimed this to be a day to be remembered forever.  What had once been merely Jill's writings was now a compelling local fable to which all the friends and relatives of the author, illustrator and speaker – and everyone else in the town – would feel a lasting personal connection. Jill's **product** was an instant classic, firmly part of the beloved local folklore. Sales were brisk at the event and will likely continue for generations to come. Because Jill created such a brilliant total **product**, only a little **publicity** (the launch) was required for marketing success.

You might think about spin-offs and add-ons to your book that could make it part of a larger 'product line'. How about:
- having the cover or a key message from your book printed on a T-shirt, to start a **movement** (possibly produce and sell the T-shirt through CafePress.com or Printfection.com),
- creating a **seminar** or night school course based on your textbook (and be paid to talk about your favorite topic),
- donating a portion of your royalties to a charity who will sell your book as their **fundraiser**,

- releasing an **eBook** version to make your book part of a multi-edition launch,
- make an **audio book** version for all those commuters tied up in traffic, and the visually challenged, or
- offering a free sample chapter in PDF format from your own **website** – then after buying your book, the customer will receive monthly newsletters of updates and other information on your topic, so the customer is buying into a **flow of up-to-date information** from an expert.

If you have aspirations of selling rights to a merchandizing company, the test-marketing of some spin-off items from your book will provide some tangible research results to show them.

Consider also that publishing a book can dramatically change a related product or service. Ross Shafer is a six-time Emmy Award-winning comedian and TV host. He regularly gives keynote speeches at conferences and he coaches the sales teams for major corporations. Yet, Ross knew something was missing from his total offering – people expected him to have a book.

Ross chose to independently publish because he could control the content, design and distribution, while meeting a tight timeline. *Nobody Moved Your Cheese!* [ISBN 1553956583] is Ross's wacky spoof on the self-help industry. Now, when responding to corporate event planners, Ross sends a sampler video plus a copy of his hilarious book. Many corporate event planners want attendees to have a gift souvenir – and the star presenter's book is a natural giveaway. Of course, Ross is happy to sell hundreds of copies at a time to the event sponsor!

Ross's book became an important part of a larger **product** and can be used as a **publicity** tool and a **sales promotion**.

Fifteen years ago, when Michael Losier wanted to become a public speaker and motivational trainer, he had lunch with a mentor who advised, "It is tough to be a successful speaker without a book."

Michael kept that in mind as he progressed through teaching small groups in his home, to training hundreds of people at a time via telephone conference calls and seminars around the world. Before he published his book, for a year he had its cover image showing on his website with a form to collect names of those wanting it. When he self-published in 2003, 1,700 copies were sold overnight to people on that list.

Michael's presentations and his book, *The Law of Attraction* [ISBN 9780973224009], soon formed an intertwined single product with each component boosting the other. That product package now includes audio CDs and DVDs, and training for people who wish to teach the Law of Attraction themselves. At a seminar, Michael may train as many as 800 people at once, and then sell 800 copies of his book. He conducted 110 seminars during 2006.

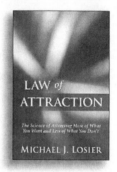

In four years, using the attraction techniques himself, Michael sold more than 250,000 copies and appeared four times on Oprah Winfrey's radio show. He attracted a publishing contract from Grand Central Publishing (Warner Books) for a hardcover edition to be translated into 28 languages. Recently he became a regular expert on Oprah's radio show.

Michael's advice on producing a book product? "My book was really the teaching manual for my seminars. I had an 8-inch stack of notes that I condensed into 100 pages for the book. Present your material in a way that appeals to all learning styles. Use short chapters that include personal anecdotes and real-life examples, with helpful illustrations to clarify your information."

Perhaps you are considering creating a new book and want to check out the sales success of competing books in that genre. You can estimate overall sales by checking at Amazon.com and Barnes & Noble's www. BN.com. Both websites show sales ranks of books they offer. More sales performance info about specific titles can be gathered at salesrankexpress. com, created by Aaron Shepard, indie author of the brilliant book *Aiming at Amazon* [ISBN 9780938497431]. Another site for comparing sales results is www.TitleZ.com.

Here's a way of interpreting the Amazon *average* sales rankings over time, according to Arthur Wait of TitleZ. Remember that a low ranking is what you are aiming for:

- Less than 100: Bestseller. Author, publisher, agent are all getting rich.
- 101 to 1000: Extremely good performer. Any publisher/author would be thrilled.
- 1001 to 10,000: Very successful book. A few of these can sustain a small publishing company.
- 10,001 to 50,000: A successful book by most industry standards.
- 50,001 to 100,000: Not bad.
- 100,000 to 500,000: Not good.
- 500,000 or more: This book definitely needs help with its marketing mix!
- no ranking: no copies have been sold from this vendor.

A final note about having an excellent product: seriously consider hiring a professional editor – someone with experience editing books for trade publishers. Years later you might look back at the investment of $3,000 to $10,000 as money *very* well spent.

CHAPTER 3

Place (distribution and timing)

---

*How, where and when will you provide your
product or service?*

I n this chapter, we'll explore a number of sales channels including these:

- within the book trade (discussing standards, distributors, mark-ups/margins, selling directly to local bookstores...)
- hosting a book launch event
- selling in gift shops and other retailers
- trade shows and other large gatherings (book industry trade shows, book festivals and salons, and non-book-industry events)
- schools and other educational markets
- going to the audience
- book clubs and catalogs
- eBooks
- audio books
- special sales

- direct response advertising distribution.

SELLING WITHIN THE BOOK TRADE

Fifteen ago, a self-publishing author had limited options for book trade distribution. Distributors and bookstores were – and still are – very reluctant to accept a single title, preferring to deal with publishing companies that provide them with dozens or hundreds of titles. Today, by using an on-demand publishing service to aggregate your title with thousands of other independent titles, the author can sell through the book trade. Your distribution won't be ideal (i.e. there won't be tall stacks of your books featured at the front of every book store), but potential readers will be able to locate and order a copy. Your local bookstore can order in copies if the manager thinks they will sell.

For most indie authors, book trade distribution of POD books is accomplished through the author's publishing service having its books' digital print files stored at Lightning Source's plants in Tennessee, USA and Milton Keynes, England. Lightning Source prints up copies to match requests from retailers and distributors around the world. Lightning Source is owned by Ingram Book – the world's largest book distributor – so retailers place their orders through Ingram's usual service. Paperback and hardcover books are printed promptly, then shipped out to the retailers along with the rest of their book orders. Lightning Source opened another printing plant in Pennsylvania in 2007 and is considering opening in other locations around the world.

Amazon.com, the online mega-retailer, automatically lists books that are available through Ingram's Lightning Source. Amazon will also buy directly from a publisher or individual author through its Advantage program. The terms of the Advantage program are heavily weighted in favor of Amazon, so it is difficult for an author to make any money selling through that program. In its Marketplace program, a customer orders from Amazon (in the *used and new* listings) who relays the info and money to the publisher or other merchant who sends the book directly to the customer. Amazon also has its own print-on-demand factory, called BookSurge, now part of Amazon's CreateSpace.com subsidiary. If a book's PDF print file is stored at BookSurge's South Carolina plant, it can be printed there for shipping to Amazon customers.

Most publishing services offer a number of basic services to ensure a book's existence is known through the book trade (sometimes the author pays extra for each task) including the following:

- each book gets an ISBN, the international standard book number that is used as a unique identification number throughout the industry,
- the cover will have an EAN/ISBN barcode required by major distributors and most stores,
- Books-in-Print, BookData, PubStock and other industry reference databases will be informed about your book and its price, so bookstores can locate the source for ordering copies,
- Ingram and Baker & Taylor and other wholesaler/distributors are told and they, in turn, include the information in their catalogs for their bookstore clients,
- Abebooks.com, Amazon.com, Borders.com, Barnes & Noble's bn.com, Chapters.indigo.ca and other major online retailers are sent the book's metadata (information), so they can offer books to their customers,
- a webpage is created for each title, showing book cover and description, an author blurb and photo, and an excerpt, and
- key Internet search engines are told about your book's webpage.

Ready for a little historical background about 'returnable' books?

I personally feel it is important to provide new authors some perspective on the most controversial and reviled aspect of the publishing industry: returnable books. You will be making some decisions about whether to participate in this questionable practice or not. There are very real environmental and financial implications.

Before the Great Depression, books were sold by publishers to bookstores on a 'firm sale' basis – essentially on the same terms that manufacturers and their distributors sell food to grocers, hammers to hardware stores, cars to dealers, etc. A bookstore owner was expected to pay for each order of new books on receipt or within 30 days at the latest. He could only return a book if it was defectively manufactured.

When the stock market crashed in 1929 and money suddenly became tight, booksellers abruptly stopped buying new books, opting to sell their inventory on hand first. The bookstore owners were prudently conserving their cash and adopting a wait-and-see approach.

Publishers, who had warehouses of books they suddenly couldn't sell, went into panic mode. In desperation, USA-based publisher Simon & Schuster offered 'guaranteed' sales. If a bookseller would take some new books, he needn't pay anything until the book sold or 90 days were up. The book could be returned if it didn't sell within this special three-month guarantee period. Other publishers had no choice but to begin offering similar special sales terms, essentially selling on consignment.

The tactic worked quite well at salvaging some sales in a desperate time. Unfortunately, once the Depression was over, publishers couldn't agree to go back to the previous firm sale terms. The 'returnable' terms spread like a bad virus to Canada and other countries, with great long-term financial damage to the book industry.

Having books on consignment puts little onus on booksellers to order their new titles carefully. Publishers must gamble on huge print runs of books even though they ultimately may sell very few copies. All too often a second run is printed because initial bookstore orders were strong, even though the first run would have more than sufficed. A few careless large purchases by a major bookstore chain (such as Borders or Barnes & Noble in the USA or Chapters-Indigo in Canada) can bankrupt a smaller publisher. The typical percentage of returned books, depending on genre, can be between 40% and 80% of the print run! Worldwide over one billion books are overprinted each year – that's *over 2.7 million books that are trashed every day.*

This shocking waste is harmful to the environment, wasting trees and fossil fuels in printing and then in trucking the books around the continent between warehouses and retail stores and back again. Making paper is the world's second largest industrial user of fresh water, and the publishing industry is shamelessly squandering that precious, limited resource.

Returnability raises the cost and retail price for those copies that are sold – by an estimated 15% to 20%. The only ones to benefit are paper companies, printers and shippers.

Nowadays, a few publishers are taking a stand and rejecting this wasteful practice. My firm, Agio Publishing House, is proud to be one of these forward-thinking companies who only sell on non-returnable terms. We are also lobbying within the book industry to rally support so everyone will eventually switch away from this wasteful system. In this era of climate change and widespread environmental concern, it is inexcusable to blatantly overprint. *See www.BookIndustryBailout.ca for more information on returnable books.*

Unfortunately, many publishing services (AuthorHouse, Trafford, etc.) now offer to make their POD books returnable. Here's how this scheme works. The publishing service lists the book as available on returnable terms within Ingram's database. Ingram accepts books back from retailers and pays to refund the retailer. The publishing service has to pay for the retailer's refund plus a service charge. The returned book is then offered to the author to buy – but the cost of finding this copy in Ingram's vast warehouses makes this uneconomical. So the book is actually shredded and a new one is printed and sent to the author instead.

The publishing service has calculated how much money it will pay out on refunds per year per title, on average. It then adds a hefty administration fee and profit, and offers this fixed annual fee to authors. In effect, the publishing service is charging an amount that is insurance against all its costs for returns.

The practice is wasteful and, from the research I've done with authors, it has not proven to be cost-effective. Retailers simply are not keen on stocking unproven, under-promoted indie titles when they have so many mainstream titles to select from, many of which come with co-op advertising and other sales incentives. When a 'returnable' indie title does get heavily ordered – for example, when an author is to be a guest on *Oprah* – thousands of copies may be returned, forcing all other authors to bear the cost through the high insurance fee.

If you are offered a returnable option, please think hard before accepting.

What does a distributor or wholesaler do?
How does pod fit into this?

There is considerable fuzziness about the definition of, and differences between, *distributors* and *wholesalers* – you can essentially use the terms interchangeably. The primary function of a distributor is to have an inventory of books on hand to ship to a retailer when orders come in, and then accept returns. The distributor passes along payment for sales to the publisher when the retailer pays, usually after 6 or 9 months when the returnable time allowance has expired. With rare exception, a book distributor will not promote or publicize individual titles unless the publisher pays a fee for that specific sales function.

Ingram Book, the world's largest book distributor, whose network extends to tens of thousands of bookstores around the globe, stocks copies of over a million different titles in its warehouses. It also lists hundreds of thousands of on-demand published titles in its catalog. Ingram doesn't warehouse any of those POD books; it orders from its print-on-demand manufacturing subsidiary (Lightning Source Inc.) as needed to fill each order. Since the book is printed and dispatched to the retailers so promptly, generally the retailer will only notice if the sales terms for that POD title are different from the 'returnable within 90 days if unsold' norm within the industry.

An individual author cannot list a title with Lightning Source – you must go through a publishing service (such as iUniverse, Trafford, Xlibris, Agio or others) that functions as an aggregator of content for Lightning Source.

It is a bit different with Amazon.com's own print-on-demand subsidiary called CreateSpace. An individual author can go directly to CreateSpace to list a title, but that seems a bit redundant at this point, since all titles listed through Lightning Source are automatically available at Amazon, while CreateSpace-listed titles are not available through the wider Ingram distribution channels. Most industry analysts expect that CreateSpace will eventually open POD printing plants in many countries where Amazon has a strong presence. At that point, having a book listed with both Lightning Source and CreateSpace might make sense.

There are two other POD manufacturers of note: Anthony Rowe in the UK and Book on Demand GmbH (BOD.de) in Germany. Anthony Rowe's publishing clients can have their books wholesaled to the UK book trade through Gardners Books; BOD.de's publisher clients have their books wholesaled through BOD's owner, Libri, and other European wholesalers.

Note that these POD manufacturers have a fairly wide repertoire of book sizes – from 5 inches by 8 inches through to A4 or 8.5 inches by 11 inches. (In North America, width is always the first measurement for book printing.) Bindings are paperback or hardback (also called *case bound*). Over the past two years, full-color inside pages have become more common and less costly.

For non-POD books, where the indie author has paid for an offset-printed run of perhaps a few thousand copies, access to Ingram or rival distributor Baker & Taylor is very difficult. These two largest US distributors simply aren't interested in stocking a single title from a one-author publishing house (which is how they view you). These distribution behemoths only cater to established publishing houses.

There are hundreds of small, usually regionally-focused, distributors in North America and Europe. Few are willing to carrying a book for which there is not a significant promotional budget attached, since they need to believe there will be enough sales 'to make it all worthwhile' in the returnable system.

Most book distributors will decline to take on a book offered directly by an author. Here are some of the most-frequently cited reasons:

- it is costly to set up and service a new account for what will likely be a low volume of sales (compared to the account of a publisher who has many titles, both new and backlist),
- there is uncertainty about the 'quality' and 'marketability' of the book, given that there is no previous track record,
- lack of long-term continuity (will there be new titles coming every year? will the self-publisher even be in business after a year or two?), and
- ordering and accounting is often conducted with EDI (electronic data interchange) which is too complicated and costly for a one-title self-publisher to establish and maintain.

Recently Ingram decided to stem the flow of new books into its warehouses from small publishers by introducing a stocking fee of $50 per title per year. If you are an indie author wanting to set up distribution on your own, expect to pay many times that annual fee to be carried by a regional distributor.

Setting yourself up with a distributor may not make economic sense – at least not until you've test marketed your book at a local level.

Do bookstores order from distributors?
Or directly from publishers? What do libraries do?

Booksellers do both, though it varies significantly around the globe. In the USA, for example, about 90% of all books are ordered through distributors, with Ingram and Baker & Taylor accounting for a lion's share of that volume (which may explain why Ingram feels so secure that it can boldly insist on a stocking fee). Compare that with the situation in the UK where I'm told that less that 10% of books are provided from wholesalers. Clearly UK booksellers prefer to order from the publisher or from that publisher's co-op distribution warehouse (which may be shared with a few other publishers).

Booksellers know where to order a book because of information on each title that appears in the book industry's key reference databases, including Books-in-Print, BookData, PubStock and others. The single most important information item is the ISBN (International Standard Book Number) which points to the publisher, its contact info and terms.

Here's some trivia about ISBNs: Recently the world was in danger of running out of unassigned ISBNs, so the industry committee that administers the system opted to add digits, going from a 10-digit code to a 13-digit code. The new 13-digit schema conforms to the global EAN standard for identifier numbers for all types of manufactured goods, which is handy because ISBN-13 barcodes will now work at any retailer, not only in bookstores. EAN codes ordinarily have the first three digits (the prefix) identifying the country of manufacture, but that doesn't make sense for books. The industry committee's clever solution was to invent two new imaginary countries – called Bookland 1 and Bookland 2 – with corresponding prefixes of 978 and 979. All the old 10-digit ISBNs now have 978 added to the front and the final check digit is recalculated. Presto, there are now one billion new ISBNs available for all the books you are going to write!

A library can order directly from a publisher, or through a general distributor/wholesaler, or it may submit an order for many different titles to a distributor (called a *library jobber*) who specializes in library orders, such as a Baker & Taylor or Coutts Information Services (now part of Ingram Book). Most libraries prefer combining all their purchasing through a jobber to minimize the number of purchase orders and payments they must process. Libraries typically receive a 15% to 20%

discount on their purchases, which means they pay $16 to $17 for a book with a suggested retail price of $20. This discount is much less than the 40% to 45% enjoyed by retailers and the 50% to 55% required by distributors.

Sometimes books purchased by a jobber and destined for a library are diverted to a re-binding plant where the binding is reinforced or replaced, making the book more durable for years of circulation.

Selling to the chains and big-box stores

Selling to chains, such as WalMart, Costco or Target, can be an enormous challenge for a lone indie author. Expect to allow 60% discount (or more) plus you must pay the shipping to individual stores. Thus WalMart would be paying you only $4 on a book to be sold for $10. They may insist on fairly intricate EDI (electronic data interchange) capability for inventory tracking and reorders. You must be able to fill re-orders at a moment's notice, with penalties for delays. The good news is that a chain will buy on firm terms (i.e. not returnable) since they have no intention of returning any books. Those not sold quickly at the initial price are soon marked down for bargain sale.

It is extremely difficult to get the attention and interest of a chain's book buyer, since there is so much competition from agents representing larger publishers. You might wish to start with a more localized campaign and prove the market, then approach a small distributor who already has the infrastructure and contacts with the chains. With a market-proven product, you'll feel more comfortable risking your funds on a very large offset print run – which may be necessary to get your per-book cost low enough to afford the 60% discount. Plus, after seeing your test market results, the distributor and chain buyer will have more confidence about making a deal with you at all. Although your **profit** per book might be tiny, the large numbers sold and the resulting **publicity** might make this route worthwhile – worthwhile depending, of course, on your **purpose** for all this, right?

Will your local bookseller carry your book?

With rare exception, the manager of a bookstore has the authority and motivation to order in small quantities of a locally-produced book if – but only if – he or she believes that there will be sufficient sales. The corollary of that statement is that, without the very real prospect of some sales, it is unlikely the local bookstore will carry your book.

You could suggest the store stock a dozen copies on a trial basis to begin with. Reasonable terms might be as follows when the store is buying copies directly from you:

- 40% discount (i.e., the store pays $12 on a book with a recommended retail price of $20),
- payment 'net 30 days' (the store pays you within one month after receiving your invoice),
- books in good condition can be returned for a refund after 90 days if not sold (you will come in to get the books and refund money for those not sold), and
- you will personally deliver the books to the store (so the store needn't pay for shipping).

You will need to present a basic invoice/statement, then check back each month to get paid and seek re-orders. One hopes the store will sell enough of your books during the 90-day period that the manager will elect to keep any unsold books, believing they will sell later. If you do have returns, they will be in small numbers that you can sell yourself over time.

I suggest you consider that you are creating a multi-year relationship with the bookseller. It is in both parties' best interest to have your book selling strongly in the store. The bookseller is certainly hoping that your book will sell at least two dozen copies per year *ad infinitum*. This arrangement will work only if people do come to the store and buy your book. Otherwise you'll get all the books back with no payment and the manager will be most reluctant to try this again.

I recommend that, to be fair, you don't take business from the local

store by selling directly to every friend, relative and neighbor – especially at a discounted price. It is your role and responsibility to direct
some potential buyers to this store. If you can't generate significant local

---

FROM: Bruce Batchelor, Agio Publishing
        151 Howe Street, Victoria, BC V8V 4K5
        250-380-0998
        bruce.batchelor@gmail.com

TO: Sam McGee, Mac's Fireweed Bookstore
        203 Main Street, Whitehorse, YT Y1A 2B2

INVOICE AND STATEMENT			April 30, 2010
10 copies	Yukon Channel Charts ISBN 1-55212-0007	@$20.00	$200.00
	less 40%		-$80.00
	net		$120.00
	shipping		15.00
	Subtotal		$135.00
	taxes GST 6%		8.10
	Total		**$143.10**

Thank you for selling our books!

Please remit within 30 days.

Terms: • *firm sale (not refundable except for any manufacturing defect)*
          • *net-30 (payment within 30 days of receipt of this invoice)*

A typical invoice to an individual bookstore

publicity from a launch or other event, the store's selling prospects may be poor.

Don't be surprised if the bookseller decides, after selling out your original batch of books, to do the re-order through a distributor such as Baker & Taylor or Ingram. This is for their bookkeeper's convenience: having one less account in the financial system.

Working with the bookseller and the local literary community

Booksellers can create, or at least kindle, the interest and the passion that creates a best seller. So can parents, teachers, librarians, reading groups and others. The idea is to get everyone and every little thing working towards building a buzz about your book. Ask the manager about displaying the book face-out versus spine-out so potential buyers can plainly see the front cover. Request a 'shelf-talker,' which is a handwritten note taped to the shelf below your book, stating this is a staff pick or manager's recommendation.

When a bookseller personally suggests a title to customers, this practice is called 'hand-selling.' It has tremendous impact on sales. Hand-selling is so important that a publisher may give away many hundreds, even thousands, of advance reading copies (called ARCs) to bookstore buyers and staff at trade shows such as Book Expo America and the London Book Fair. Providing a complimentary ARC of your book for your local bookstore owner and his/her staff to read could be a prudent investment! Being able to take home and read an ARC is a much-appreciated perquisite for bookstore staff.

Consider having a reading and signing event in the bookstore, and a reading at the local public library. The more publicity you can stir up, the more books will be bought. The manager and your librarian can fill you in on scheduling and their expectations. Don't neglect school librarians who may be able to set up presentations to students and faculty. Book cover posters can be used to announce a signing or a reading – make sure before they are printed that there will be some blank space at the bottom where you can fill in the date, time and location.

Librarians are generally quite responsive to new book requests by their patrons, so having a few friends ask for your book could trigger a purchase by that library and maybe by affiliated branches as well.

If it is highly important to your overall purpose to have your book accessible through certain libraries without delay, consider simply donating a copy to each of these key libraries. This will ensure your book is in circulation promptly – for researchers and those in your community who can't afford to buy all the books they want to read, yet who could benefit from reading yours.

HOSTING A BOOK LAUNCH EVENT

With the right help and preparations, your book's launch could make a great first impression AND sell enough books to pay for all of your publishing costs! I encourage you to think ahead, to the moment a few months from now, when it is time to announce your newly-published book at a launch. This event can be extremely important... so important that I asked Tom Reilly, who was Trafford Publishing's managing director in Ireland, to provide a few pointers.

Here's what Tom wrote:

Launches are always happening here. There was one in the old church while I was away last week and it all went off perfectly smoothly. [I'll interrupt Tom here to explain that Trafford's office in the Irish town of Drogheda was in an old decommissioned church on the site of a medieval monastery where monks once created the famous illuminated manuscripts for Europe's nobility and upper class, using quill pens and ink. That was literally the original 'print-on-demand' process! It was a great space for a launch party, though any large room will do nicely.]

There was also an event in Kilkenny last week where a national government minister launched the book. We have one coming up in Sligo soon and one in Dublin (launch by a celebrity journalist).

Essentially, book launches are an excellent way to recover the cost of the publishing package while at the same time exposing your book to the public in your wider community. There is also a great buzz for the author as the countdown gets closer. Pre-launch press pieces as well as after-launch articles can be arranged, which gives the launch extra mileage.

Usually local papers will feature coverage of a launch and this can also lead to national media coverage in some instances as the various media need to fill spaces or airtime. Your book could well fill that gap.

It is always a good idea to ask a politician or well-known figurehead (either local or national) to perform the official launch. They love to be asked and to be seen contributing to the literary arts and the rich varied tapestry that is the written word.

Always invite a wide cross section of the community including community groups, religious organizations, writers groups, etc. People always buy books at a launch. Always invite twice as many people as you want there. Usually only half the people turn up. A good idea also is try never to have a launch at weekends as people usually 'have somewhere else to go.'

Never underestimate the power of a book launch with regard to the success of your book. It could be the catalyst that gives you your fifteen minutes of fame. And if you are really lucky it could easily last for an hour.

[Did I mention that Tom is a best-selling indie author who writes a weekly humor column for the Drogheda newspaper? Think of him as Ireland's Dave Barry. Check out his book, *Life of Reilly*, ISBN 9781412088671.]

Here's more from Tom:

Gentlepeople,

On Wednesday, we had ONE book launch here TWICE. I know that last sentence doesn't make sense, but it's true.

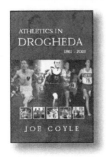

*Our author Joe Coyle [*Athletics in Drogheda, *ISBN 1412013410] made book launching history as his book had to be launched twice in one night because of the huge numbers that turned up. Joe sent out over 400 invitations for an event that was taking place in a room with a capacity of 200.*

The countdown to launch time was only ten minutes when it was suddenly realized that the booked room (upstairs) was full to capacity, while the stairs, the hall and the foyer were all packed full of people. And cars were still arriving in the car park outside. Everybody, their grannies, dogs, cats and even their imaginary friends and alter egos had decided to come.

The overflow – another 200 odd people (very odd, trust me) were hastily ushered into a separate unprepared room downstairs and waited for the first launch to be over. The principal speakers then flew downstairs, rewound and pressed play – again.

The speakers included the Mayor of Drogheda and the President of the Athletic Association of Ireland, who kindly agreed to perform their speaking duties twice, once upstairs and once downstairs. Anchor man for the evening, well-known local commentator, certified madman and Ireland office head, Tom Reilly, flew the Trafford flag by (in athletic parlance) 'running' the show and keeping both launches 'on track.'

It's a typical example of Irish eccentricity – launching a book to be sure, to be sure.

Goodbye from the Emerald Isle,

Regards, Tom Reilly

If you are considering a publishing service, ask if that company provides you with some marketing 'collateral,' such as these:

- posters, showing your book's cover in full color – to post around town or use as decorations,
- color postcards, also showing your book's cover – perfect to use as invitations,
- bookmarks, again showing your book's cover – each will show all the information someone would need to order a copy of your book by phone, post, email or web,
- business cards – with your contact info, and a photo of the book cover and ordering information,
- a press release sheet,
- a free-standing banner or large poster, and
- copies of your book – to pass out as advance reading copies to the local media or to sell at the event.

The first launch event I ever attended was back in 1975, in the Yukon, and it was to celebrate my first self-published book. I rented the Porter Creek hall, hired a square dance caller, asked a friend to play rock 'n' roll tunes during the caller's breaks, and invited friends to bring food for a potluck feast. I vaguely remember buying two or three kegs of beer to lubricate the crowd. Over two hundred people showed up and danced until dawn.

No one asked me to read from my book. Yet everyone had so much fun that for months afterward they were urging me to write a sequel! And I was now generally referred to as a 'local author' and everyone knew about – and many bought – my book. Over thirty years later, *Yukon Channel Charts* [ISBN 978155212000] is still in print and brings in a seemingly perpetual trickle of royalties.

One of my **purposes** in publishing that book was to have a big launch party to thank all my friends. In my case, the launch was not great for selling copies (I hadn't brought any along) but it was excellent for **publicity**.

What about **place**? My self-published *Yukon Channel Charts* regularly sold 500 copies *every* summer through Whitehorse gift shops, bookstore and outfitters. My only 'work' was to bring them boxes of books each spring and pick up their payment. When I eventually moved away from the Yukon, one bookstore bought out the remainder of my print run (a four years' supply) and paid cash on the spot. No wonder I came to be convinced that self-publishing could be simple, fun and rewarding! I had the only up-to-date map book of the Whitehorse-to-Dawson river route (a unique **product**) and only needed to get it into the right **places** – Whitehorse stores at the start of that popular canoe and rafting trip.

Victoria author Frank Keeling organized a reading/launch party with the owners of a local pub/restaurant and a bookstore to promote his autobiographical account of childhood sexual abuse [*Nobody's Son*, 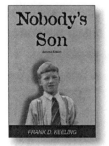 ISBN 1552124991]. Both establishments promoted this literary evening in their newsletters, flyers and ads, while Frank arranged publicity with local newspapers and radio, and invited family and friends. The owners of the Blethering Place pub were happy to have extra customers buying meals and drinks on an otherwise slow evening, while a staff member from Ivy's Bookstore was on hand to sell books. Frank read passages of his book with such conviction that even the pub regulars were intrigued and bought copies.

Frank Keeling told me he wanted to read publicly from his book (**purpose**), in part as a cathartic process and in part to experience the satisfaction of being like Frank McCourt at a literary festival reading *Angela's Ashes*. He found the right venue (**place**), secured **publicity** and established **partnerships** with a pub and a bookseller. I've now heard both Franks perform and thought our Mr. Keeling did the superior job.

Selling in gift shops and to other retailers

If your book would make an obvious gift, or is a useful resource, consider offering it to retailers outside the book trade. A local history or guide book might be a natural for sales at hotel counters or restaurants. If there is sufficient tourist traffic, you might have a steady 'cash cow' on your hands.

Publishers Weekly reported that author Robert Dorr sold an incredible 13,200 copies of his book, *Hell Hawks: The Untold Story of the American Fliers Who Savaged Hitler's Wehrmacht* [ISBN 978-0760329184], in less than two years through one store – the bookstore/gift shop of an aviation museum at Washington Dulles Airport. The **place** is ideal (teeming with tourists seeking a souvenir) and Robert adds an essential **personal sales** touch by spending between three to eight hours every day in the store greeting potential customers and pitching his book. Is there an ideal location for *your* book?

If you do have a new book in mind with an obvious ideal sales location, it makes financial sense to self-publish rather than offer the title to a mainstream publisher or use a publishing service. You will be orchestrating most of the sales yourself and deserve to reap the monetary rewards for doing so. Using a publisher your author royalty might be 10% to 15% of the retail price. As a self-publisher you could easily double that margin, and put thousands of dollar more per year in your pocket.

When selling to gift stores and other retailers outside the book trade, terms are generally 50% off the retail price on a 'firm sale' basis (versus 40% off to a bookstore on returnable or consignment terms).

Imagine where potential buyers for your book will be, and see if the proprietor is game to try selling some copies. Merchants can be keen on earning a few dollars more from each client on an impulse purchase near the checkout. If your book comes equipped with an EAN ISBN-13 barcode on the back cover, it is ready for the cashier to scan. The merchant may sticker over with any retail price that you and he/she agree upon.

Generally the mass market paperback rack in a grocery store or drug store will be stocked by a supplier who leases the space, provides the books and splits the proceeds of sales with the retailer. Such a supplier is called a 'rack jobber.' If you can interest a jobber in carrying your title, that agreement could see your book displayed in dozens, even hundreds of stores. Jobbers will want a steep discount (at least 55%, likely 65%) since they have to split that discount with the retailer, and might want the first lot of books on a consignment basis. If you are doing a consignment sale, be careful to stipulate that you want the whole book returned in saleable condition – not only the ripped-off cover that jobbers typically send back for credit!

Working with a rack jobber, if your book proves popular and is selling strongly to the stores' customers, you'll be in a position to renegotiate the discount percentage for subsequent batches.

TRADE SHOWS AND OTHER LARGE GATHERINGS

Could your book be sold or promoted effectively at book fairs, expositions, festivals, salons and trade shows? What are the bonus paybacks for selling or promoting your book at these large events? What can you expect to happen? Is exhibiting right for everyone? How about paying someone else to display your book?

Let's start by dividing events into a few categories. This will help you decide what might be appropriate for your marketing mix.

Book industry trade shows

Book Expo America, the London Book Fair and the huge Frankfurter Buchmesse are examples of the largest shows. There are also many significant book industry trade shows in Mexico, Japan, India, Singapore and other regions around the world.

These are events designed for publishers to promote upcoming titles to bookstore staff and buyers, and for publishers and agents to hammer out deals for foreign language editions and movie rights. The general public is not encouraged to attend – in fact, the admission price is usually set prohibitively high, to discourage those not employed in the trade.

Big name authors are on hand to autograph hundreds (sometimes thousands) of free copies (called ARCs or advance reading copies) that are given to bookstore staff to encourage them to 'hand sell' (personally recommend) the new book to their clientele. There is much hoopla and colorful competition among publishing houses as each tries to impress the delighted retail clerks and buyers. Sometimes wine and food are offered at publishers' booths to thank loyal merchants. Industry association meetings and seminars are held in rooms adjacent to the exhibition hall.

Some 'shopping' is being done by film producers and foreign-language publishers who are looking for marketable products and ideas. Almost all deals, though, have been developed in the months prior, with a meeting at the show intended for shaking hands, signing the contract and possibly impressing some journalists. You can't count on getting anyone's attention if you are an unknown new author, but it is fun to see the top celebrities of the book world on stage and walking by.

Could your book inspire a made-for-TV movie or maybe a children's toy? Is it a natural for translation? Maybe you could put yourself on the pathway to these opportunities by attending. If you want to exhibit at one of these annual trade shows, consider sharing costs for a booth with other authors. If you are using a publishing service, ask them about joining their contingent.

Do not expect to sell copies of your book at an industry expo – most exhibitors do not even have a cashier. The norm is passing out those ARCs or, at minimum, a brochure/info sheet. You might also bring postcards and bookmarks to distribute, plus posters to decorate the booth.

A real bonus to sharing space with others is that you can spell off one another, taking time to explore and learn. For most of us writers, a book expo is a wonderland where everyone *loves* books and authors are the stars. You may see celebrities like Bill Clinton and Margaret Atwood autographing ARCs – their name tag says 'AUTHOR' just like yours does.

Is this a good place to land a contract with a large publishing house? Yes and no. First, realize that most of the publishing staff are there to push their own new titles, not to look for next year's product. Yet there will be many acquisition editors and literary agents attending, and you may be able to interest one or two in taking a complimentary copy of your book to read later. After that, it is the quality of your writing and its fit with the publisher's 'list' that could prompt a contract offer.

Will book buyers from retail stores seek you out? It is unlikely you'll get any interest if you sit behind a table all day! Buyers are generally overwhelmed with tens of thousands of choices. You'll need to be circulating and actively chatting up everyone you meet, repeating your concise sales pitch hundreds of times a day and passing out bookmarks and flyers – hoping to endear yourself to at least a few bookstore clerks and buyers.

Mary Lucas, publicist at Trafford Publishing, had this reaction to attending book expos: "It was an incredible experience to be surrounded by industry professionals. The knowledge I gained from conversations with distributors, agents, librarians and booksellers was invaluable. What a great opportunity for authors to deliver the sales pitch for their books! We had literally hundreds of people stopping at our booth to learn more about the books we were exhibiting.

"After Book Expo in Chicago in 2004, our author Valentine Brkich reported that a Random House editor would be reading his book [*Cageball, Poker and the Atomic Wedgie: A Tale of Catholic School Mischief*, ISBN 1412005744] on her flight back to New York. A representative from Disney had a chat with Tom Abbondandolo and Ted Kole about the artwork created by Greek Princess Marie in the book called *A Tale Of Katoufs: From Royal Times To Nursery Rhymes* [ISBN 1412027624]. And after the 2004 Book Expo Canada, authors Kim Tait, Mary Pendlebury and Maria Van Santen-Almudevar all reported positive interest in their titles from editors and literary agents. Ron Coleman lined up sales agreements with a number of bookstores for his book, *Just Watch Me: Trudeau's Tragic*

Legacy [ISBN 155395565X] and consultant Paul Thompson [*Small Business Sucks... but it doesn't have to* [ISBN 1552123928] was booked for a few lucrative speaking engagements."

What is a common theme to these personal experiences and successes? It is that none of these opportunities involved directly selling a single copy of a book at the fair. Book industry shows are for networking, learning and creating opportunities.

Harley Melton, author of *Touch Not This Wall: A Novel of the Vietnam War... and After* [ISBN 1412044189], who was at the 2005 Book Expo America, provides this perspective for authors considering attending a future book expo:

"Don't expect that droves of people will stop and literally snatch a copy of your work from your hands. And the publishers are there to sell their goods to booksellers and see what the other guys have, not to pick up books from other publishers or authors.

"But, there is a great positive for *any* author attending BEA. It is a rare, an extremely rare, opportunity to be face-to-face with publisher executives who might, just might, be interested enough in you and your work to take you on, if not for your current work, for your future work(s).

"I would suggest that other authors do as I did," says Harley. "Research the list of publishers that are slated to attend, pick about twenty to twenty-five who publish your genre/theme and start from one end of the building and work your way to the other. Most were kind enough to give me a few minutes to present my nonfiction book; only one told me that they don't publish conservative crap (not the word he used but very close). Of the twenty publishers I had pre-selected, four in particular seemed to be more than just polite."

Book festivals, fairs and salons

There are hundreds of these literary celebrations, large and small. Examples are the Baltimore Book Fair, Miami Book Fair, the Word-on-the-Street events in many Canadian cities, and the fabulous Salons du livre in the province of Québec. At these events, the audience is the general public and most exhibitors' aim is to sell books to them.

ARCs and promotional copies are rare – because no exhibitor could afford to give away tens of thousands of free books! When school children attend in large numbers, as happens at the salons, giving away autographed bookmarks is common. Though still expensive, most publishers consider this promotion as a long-term investment in their authors' career.

Check with organizers about rules for selling; sometimes a local business license is required. One option is to collect orders (recording the buyer's credit card details, address and phone number) that will be mailed later to the buyer's home. If you are selling for cash, it can be convenient and motivating to round down the price to an even figure. For example, you could be saying, "We have a show special. My book retails for $24.95. If you buy today, it is an even $20.00."

Sharing booth space with other authors will reduce your expenses, plus you'll meet some creative, like-minded people. For booth decorations, posters of your book's cover will come in handy. Consider the investment of a few hundred dollars for a portable, lightweight, free-standing banner and other professional signage. Companies such as Displays2go.com and SDsign.com offer many portable signage choices.

Les salons du livre, a series of nine regional book fairs across the province of Québec, are amazing events for any bibliophile. Typically smaller book fairs in Anglophone (English-speaking) North America are sparsely attended by the general public even with no or minimal admission fees; the focus is almost entirely on books, and books must be offered at a bargain price to achieve some sales. By contrast, *les salons* attract a large portion of the regional population who pay up to $10 each per day to tour publishers' exhibits; they watch all manner of live theatre and other boisterous cultural entertainment, and stand in long line-ups to purchase large quantities of books at full retail price.

Schoolchildren arrive in long bus convoys, thousands joyously swarming through the exhibit areas, anxious to get an autograph from their favorite young-adult authors. Writers are adored celebrities whose interviews and panel discussions are broadcast over local and provincial radio and TV, and featured in newspaper and magazine special inserts. If you get an opportunity to attend a *salon du livre* and can speak French, I recommend it. Walt Disney couldn't create a better fantasyland for authors!

Non-book-industry events

Some independent authors exhibit at such diverse gatherings as a dentists' trade show, a horse show and a religious gathering. The great advantages for an author include:

- the audience has an obvious interest in a specific subject, so they are 'pre-qualified leads' for an author of a book on that subject,
- there will be few (if any) other exhibitors selling books, and
- since you are a subject-matter expert, organizers may pay you to attend and present a seminar or make a speech.

Events are great for arranging new non-bookstore sales channels. See if other exhibitors want to sell your book in their stores or mail-order businesses. Talk to exhibitors and other attendees about buying books for incentives or to combine into a 'package' with their products.

When you find a gathering that matches your book well, not only will you sell copies, but you'll also be meeting people who are sincerely interested in you and your book's theme. For authors who are retired and have time for a bit of traveling, attending specialty events can become a delightful annual pilgrimage. Even if you don't recover all your costs, your accountant may advise you to claim the rest as a tax-deductible business expense.

Paul "Buck" Kalinowski, Jr. from Wolcott, Connecticut, wrote two children's books, called *Cupid's Secret* and *The Adventures of Arrow* [ISBN 1412047439 and 155369595X], which he sells from his ranch, 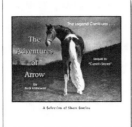 through a website (www.cupidandarrow.com) and also at horse shows. Buck is a singer who often entertains at the shows, which draws further attention to his award-winning horses (Cupid and Arrow) and their namesake books.

Buck has assembled a **product** line of porcelain models, plush toys and beanie horses fashioned in the horses' likeness, eBook versions, CDs and T-shirts – so he can cross-market. He has hired scriptwriters to create a movie proposal. His book sales are over 20,000 copies and steadily climbing.

Buck has figured out his **public** very well, and has nailed the best **place**s to sell his books as well – his ranch, website and horse events.

Burt S. Levy, who wrote and self-published the acclaimed auto racing novel *The Last Open Road* [ISBN 096421072X], is another master at 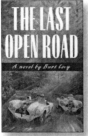 event selling.

"My experience is that exhibitions are *alternatives* for book sales," says Burt. "Not so much *instead* of the traditional bookstore market, but *in addition* to it. And once again, it comes down to identifying and focusing in on your core market and figuring out where and how you can access them. In our case, we did far better with gift shops and souvenir stands at racetracks and museums, doing book signings at major races, auctions and car nut events, and getting featured in specialty catalogues that sold everything from car polish to brake linings. In most cases, we were the only book featured. Or at least the only novel. But it sold copies, spread the word, and most importantly, made money for our retailers as well as ourselves. That's key, because they're not going to want you around if you're not ringing the old cash register."

The Last Open Road is now, 16 years after its launch, still finding new readers worldwide and is heading into its 7th printing with over 40,000 copies sold. It has also evolved into a four-novel series (plus a short story anthology) with total sales in excess of $1 million.

Burt's books continue to sell well at racetracks. As he proclaims on his www.lastopenroad.com website, "Burt will be shamelessly hawking and signing books at:" and then he lists upcoming racetrack events he'll be attending. Burt delightfully admits to a passion for 'mooching' rides in the fastest race cars. There is no doubt this author is having a carload of fun while being very successful selling his books.

Clearly, the amount of money you'll be netting from in-person sales depends on how much you are paying for copies of your book from a printer or a publishing service. If you figure that personal sales at events will be a key part of your marketing mix, devote special attention to printing costs when selecting a publishing service or a printer. If you'll be taking advantage of print-on-demand, you can order as many copies as required at any time, and have them shipped directly to the exhibition site or your hotel.

Are you looking to have your book on display at professional as-sociation conferences and other trade shows, but can't justify the cost to take yourself there and rent exhibit space? There are two services in the USA who can help. For a fee, your book can be part of a joint exhibit with many publishers. Discovering a book at a conference could prompt a professor to adopt it as a course text – that's like winning a multi-year lottery for a publisher because sales will happen every school semester until that professor retires. The cost to use an exhibit service for only one show is about $60 per title, but that per-title, per-show price drops dramatically as you commit to more shows and/or have more titles.

Check out my favorite, Association Book Exhibit at www.BookExhibit.com, phone Mark Trocchi at 703-619-5030 or info@bookexhibit.com. Also hosting group booths is Combined Book Exhibit at www.CombinedBook.com, phone 914-739-7500 or info@combinedbook.com.

Schools and other educational markets

At first glance, the educational market looks so easy: a steady turnover of students needing over-priced texts, and college bookstores requiring only 15% to 25% margin. Further investigation shows why this can actually be a very tough market.

Professors expect free evaluation copies (called 'desk copies'), which creates a significant expense. The major educational publishers will routinely send out thousands of desk copies of a new text or edition, hoping it will catch on somewhere, then dispatch salesmen to follow up. Professors considering a new text have come to expect free teaching guides and audio-visual materials – even test questions.

Selection of the course text will not be an impartial evaluation. A major educational publishing house will usually recruit a half-dozen professors (each prominent at a major university) to co-author a text because each professor can be relied on to ensure the new book will be compulsory for thousands of students taking that subject at his/her university.

Some professors will create a 'course pack,' which is a compilation of the professor's own writings and copied sections from other texts, custom-printed by the campus print shop or through a publishing service. If you are that professor, good for you – you have the **place** for sales in the bag!

So how does an outsider break into the educational market? It will take persistence and personal contact with key decision-makers at each campus. The best news is that there is considerable inertia within the academic world – once your book becomes the recommended text and a professor builds his or her lectures and exams around it, your book could enjoy a tenure measured in decades (until the professor retires!) and thousands of copies sold.

Selling to elementary or high schools generally involves having your book endorsed or approved by a state or provincial committee. This process can take years, with no guarantee local school boards will adopt your text. If you are an insider (professor, teacher or educational consultant), these screening processes can work in your favor because you will have connections within the system that competitors may lack.

Marketing Engineering: Computer-Assisted Marketing Analysis and Planning [ISBN 9781412022521] is a combination of textbook, software and business cases developed and written by Penn State professors Gary L. Lilien and Arvind Rangaswamy. The three components of their **product** are intended to be used together to provide theory (textbook), computer modeling techniques (software) and context-specific operations decisions and action (business cases).

In keeping with academic expectations, the price tag is a hefty $124. Gary and Arvind are using their professional network to encourage adoption in business schools around the world. Because of their impressive credentials and reputations (**positioning**) and the nature of their **product**, the academic world is definitely the **place** for their marketing focus.

GOING TO THE AUDIENCE

Can you visualize a beautiful target audience and go to the beautiful place where they are?

In 2002, Patricia and Dr. Harv Haakonson decided to devote a year to traveling around North America in a new motorhome, promoting their two self-published books [*Easy Low Carb Cooking* – ISBN 9781550226812 and *Slow Carb for Life – The*

Ultimate Practical Guide to Low-Carb Living – ISBN 9781550226805].
A typical foray into each town would include golfing and being lunch-time guest speakers at the local high-end golf course, followed by pre-arranged media interviews and an autographing event in the local book-store. Next day would see them golfing with, and speaking to, more rich Baby Boomers in the next town.

Their media scrapbook was soon bulging. The *Winnipeg Free Press* dubbed them 'The Low-Carb Missionaries.' As they traveled to spread their slow-carb gospel, they were setting up bookstore accounts. Sales were significant – over ten thousand copies of each book were sold be-fore two publishing houses began bidding to sign a contract with Patricia and Harv. The Haakonsons chose a multi-book deal with ECW Press in the summer of 2004 to continue promoting their lifestyle. Harv and Pa-tricia regularly appear on TV shows discussing topics such as teen obe-sity and 'the 10 biggest mistakes dieters make.'

When the Haakonsons examined their **purpose**, it seemed natural that their own lifestyle choices were paramount if they were to be advo-cating change for others. They became the embodiment of the successful couple – articulate, trim, athletic, rich, purposeful, able to travel – which is **positioning** or branding. They took their show on the road in delight-ful fashion, going to their audience at some of the loveliest golf courses in the world (**place**). That's quite an enviable marketing mix solution.

BOOK CLUBS AND CATALOGS

Depending on its genre, your book might be saleable through a mail-order catalog company. There are thousands of catalog companies, the most famous example being the Book-of-the-Month Club. Scholar's Bookshelf is another well-known vendor, selling an impressive quantity of baseball and military titles.

Typically, a catalog based on a certain theme (e.g., baseball, military history, knitting, crime fiction, etc.) is mailed to a well-targeted list of potential customers, who order either by return mail or phone. Although in recent years Internet promotions and responses have cut significantly into sales through these mailed catalogs, there are apparently still about 7,000 different catalogs published in the USA alone, accounting for over 11 billion pieces mailed every year!

Check out www.buyersindex.com and your local library for lists of catalog companies, then explore which ones cater to an audience that matches your book's niche market. You'll need to send a free review copy and a pitch letter explaining why you expect their catalog to be a good fit. Wait for a reply before suggesting terms since they can vary quite a bit: 50% versus 60% discount, payment in 30 days versus 6 months, and firm sale versus consignment basis.

Because of the time required to prepare, print and mail catalogs, there is generally a lead time of four to six months between making a deal and knowing if any catalog recipients are keen about buying your book. Generally a few titles are featured, and up to a hundred more are presented in smaller listings. The good news is that, if there is a good response, you may be selling dozens of copies every time the catalog is mailed out – and the catalog company will keep offering your book forever. That's a great passive income stream.

eBooks

In the mid-1990s, many experts predicted that eBooks would soon make printed-on-paper books obsolete. In 2000, analyst firm Andersen Consulting predicted over $2 billion annually in eBook sales within five years. Ten years later, eBook sales still haven't reached that level but are growing rapidly every year. The introduction of Amazon's Kindle, Sony's Reader, Barnes & Noble's Nook and Apple's iPad have certainly publicized the concept of reading books on a portable device.

Sales of electronic editions of popular books are happening in many ways and formats, including files that can be read on ordinary personal computers, handhelds and cell phones.

While the world awaits the perfect reading device, some mainstream publishers are investing heavily to make more eBook content available. For example, Harlequin, publisher of the famous *Harlequin Romance* series, is now releasing 80 to 100 eBook titles every month.

Lest anyone argue that eBooks will never impose a threat to the sale of paper books, consider the fate of printed encyclopedias. Only twenty years ago, most middle-class families owned an impressive row of hard-bound encyclopedia volumes from venerable sources such as Encyclopaedia Britannica (founded 1768), Encyclopedia Americana (1829) or Funk & Wagnalls (1876). Within a half-decade though, those printed

books were rendered redundant by free or inexpensive reference CDs from Microsoft's *Encarta* and others. Those CDs, in turn, have been replaced by online searches at Google. com and Wikipedia.org. Perhaps consumers are not so fixated with the smell of ink, the texture of leather bindings and the joy of turning pages as some in the book industry would have us all believe. As the right devices, formats and online shops are available for eBook reading, print book sales in many genres may quickly migrate to the new media.

Jeff Paleczny holds an iRex Iliad book reader that uses e-ink technology

Several electronic book sales initiatives hold promise for extra royalty income to authors, and these programs also provide valuable extra exposure for your book. Google's Book Search program (www.books.google.com) allows people to read parts of any book that Google can get its hands on (you or your publishing service can send them a printed or PDF copy to expedite this). Google will soon provide a mechanism for people to subscribe or buy rights to read all of your book online. If your book is part of their program, you'll be receiving royalties.

Meanwhile Amazon has its Search Inside™ feature (customers can browse through your book's pages) and Kindle (you can sign up to have your book available as an eBook, and set the price). Amazon gives the (self-) publisher a respectable 70% of the retail price collected on Kindle sales. Smashwords.com is a handy service for making your book available through dozens of eBook channels (including cell phones), and they keep only 15% of your royalty for doing all the format conversions and legwork.

While I was running Trafford, a few dozen authors experimented by offering their books in eBook PDF format. Are you wondering which titles sold best? Not surprisingly it was the non-fiction, niche books packed with how-to information on, for example, Internet security, obesity surgery or investing. Sales for fiction and poetry were particularly rare – for some titles, *no* copies were ever sold. It seems that some people want specific practical information *right now* and are okay with squinting at a computer screen, while those wanting to savor the entertainment prefer to read an old-fashioned printed book.

Do you have a fiction title and want some world-wide exposure to an audience that is currently heavily weighted to teenaged girls who read books in installments on their cell phones? You can easily share your writings and gain feedback and suggestions from readers at Wattpad. com. Wattpad is now the world's most popular ebook community, delivering billions of pages from its library of over 250,000 eBooks created by the community. Wattpad receives 10 million monthly visits on its websites and mobile applications. With over 5 million downloads, Wattpad is also the most widely-used mobile eBook application in the world. Some authors are regularly attracting over a million 'page views' of their stories. Although all books are read free on Wattpad, experiments are underway to see how an author can leverage a worldwide fan base into sales of the printed book.

Currently the vast majority of content is un-edited young adult fiction, but this could soon change. Agio Publishing House authors are collaborating with Wattpad's CEO Allen Lau to introduce well-polished books in true crime and other genres, hoping to build a more diverse user-base for Wattpad while boosting awareness of our authors' books. Each chapter/episode will have links to purchasing the print editions.

In the spring of 2010, accomplished author Barry Mathias will begin releasing episodes through Wattpad of *The Power in the Dark: Book One of The Ancient Bloodlines Trilogy* [ISBN 9781897435113] to see how well this exposure will generate sales of the print versions of the other two books in the trilogy, which will not be available for free on Wattpad.

Barry's strategy reminds me of how encyclopedias were marketed in the 1960s. The first volume – covering the letter 'A' – would be offered in the grocery store for free or very inexpensively to get the family 'hooked' on this 'limited time offer.' Then subsequent volumes would be offered, one every two weeks, at a much higher price. This approach was very successful to sell encyclopedias – my parents bought the full set of *Funk & Wagnalls Encyclopedia* this way for their four children to use – and time will tell if offering free eBooks will bring similar book sales success.

The many authors who have been concerned about piracy will be encouraged to learn that the actual rate of piracy incidents reported to eBook vendors and distributors is quite low.

I believe it is important to build the geographical range and variety of ways one's content is available to readers – as long as offering all this varied distribution is not itself overly costly. My invention of print-on-demand publishing in the mid-1990s has opened access to the book trade for hundreds of thousand of independent authors. The mainstream publishing houses are also gradually adopting the POD approach to cut their costs and keep back-list titles in print. A similar quantum shift is beginning to happen now with the growing selection of lower-cost eBook content, good margins for publishers, fair royalties for authors, and ergonomically-pleasing mechanisms for reading/viewing books.

Intrinsically, the eBook concept is far better for our environment than printed books – an eBook only uses recycled electrons! With the reality of global climate change upon us, we all need to support eBook sales growth. If you have a viable way to include your indie book in the steadily-growing eBook content pool, please do so!

AUDIO BOOK SALES

An audio book can be thought of as a book that is read to you. Sales of these sound recordings constitute one of the most rapidly-growing segment of the book trade. The increase isn't terribly surprising when one considers the hundreds of millions of people worldwide spending long hours each day commuting to and from work. Then add in all the time people have to fill while working out in gyms or doing other activities. Plus our aging population has so many people with vision challenges.

Audio books were once sold as vinyl record albums, which were replaced by cassette tapes, then CDs and then DVDs. The most recent trend has been to the MP3 and AAC formats used for digital downloaded music – eliminating the need for the DVD or other physical media altogether. Rather than buying a tall stack of cassettes or a half-dozen CDs, the buyer simply downloads the entire spoken book from websites such as www. audible.com (owned by Amazon) or Apple Inc.'s iTunes Store at www. apple.com/itunes/store/audiobooks.html.

Across the industry, according to a July 2006 *New York Times* article by Motoko Rich (*'Authors Take a New Approach to Audio Books: Do It Yourself'*), an audio book edition can be expected to bring in about 10 percent of the revenue realized from hardcover sales.

How big is the audio book market? According to the Audio Publishers Association, "nearly 25% of the US population is listening to audio books, and audio book sales in 2006 increased 6% to reach $923 million." Of course, the audio book industry registered a huge sales boost when the *Harry Potter* books came out in audio editions.

About 14% of audio book sales were in purely digital download form (i.e. no CD or DVD or cassettes) in 2006. That percentage almost tripled between 2004 and 2006, so it is likely about 50% now.

In creating an audio book, the narrator could be an accomplished actor or other 'talent,' or the author. Depending on the publisher's vision, the production could be elaborate with multiple voices, sound effects and music, or it could be a single voice recorded with one microphone. Audio editing could be intensive to eliminate every single rustle of paper or poor inflection – or it could allow for a more natural flow with some stumbling and the occasional cough or throat clearing.

If professional talent is hired and extensive editing is mandated, the overall production cost will quickly run into many tens of thousands of dollars. Skilled actors are typically paid from $4,000 to $6,000 to perform a 6-hour audio book. No wonder publishers feel compelled to set the price at over $60 for a CD set, or $35 for a download – for a book whose hardcover edition didn't cost that much!

An independent author intent on producing an elaborate audio book of his or her opus can hire a recording studio and engineer, expecting to pay about $5,000 for a fairly polished product. Unfortunately the average author would have little chance of recovering a tenth of that in sales.

Of course, some indie authors are determined, inventive and extremely frugal! Those indie authors are discovering that a good USB microphone ($80) and some audio editing software are all the tools required to create their own audio book. It will take a month of evenings to read, re-read and edit a book by yourself. A free software application for recording and editing on a PC is Audacity, available at http://audacity. sourceforge.net/. Those using Macintosh computers will have a program called GarageBand already installed.

The twin challenges in *marketing* the resulting audio book are similar to those faced when marketing a printed book: they are *awareness* and *availability*. Some enterprising indie authors are promoting and selling their audio books directly to customers at their own websites, as downloads or on CDs, eschewing elaborate anti-piracy measures.

Currently the main retail sites for downloadable audio books – iTunes and Audible.com – are not set up to accept books from individual self-publishing authors, though you can attempt to establish a distribution agreement when you have four or more titles. Audible is the exclusive supplier of audio book titles to the iTunes store so getting on Audible automatically lists your audio book with Apple's popular store. Unfortunately, the royalty or margin percentage passed on by Audible to publishers is disappointingly low – something that surely will improve as competition increases.

To sell an audio book in MP3 format on a CD, indie authors can go to CreateSpace.com which will list the book on Amazon.com and manufacture the CD in a plastic 'jewel' case on demand.

Although audio book sales may be modest now, my publishing company is encouraging our authors to create audio books editions, believing that the marketplace is surely going to keep growing as eyesight gradually deteriorates for those in the baby boomer generation. As well, there must be potential for audio book sales growth to a younger audience based on survey findings that over half of all North American teens now own an MP3 player.

One promising development for indie authors is the increasing popularity of 'podiobooks' as available at www.podiobooks.com. These are books recorded as chapter episodes by the author and available as podcasts to readers. Some readers pay a donation, while others may buy the printed edition after being captivated by the audio episodes.

Matthew Wayne Selznick is an author, freelance editor, expert podcaster and musician. Since October 2004, he's produced regular podcasts featuring independent music from around the world. The podcasts are essentially short radio programs, recorded in his home studio, and distributed free across the Internet for people to listen on their computers or iPods. Matthew's show is called the *DIY Endeavors Podcast*.

As a self-proclaimed evangelist for the DIY (do it yourself) ethic, it was natural that Matthew chose to handle by himself nearly every aspect of the publishing and marketing of his sci-fi book.

In November 2004, Matthew's *Brave Men Run – A Novel of the*

Sovereign Era was the very first novel to be simultaneously released as a paperback [ISBN 141165661X, printed by Lulu.com], eBook in five formats and free podcast.

"I've been very verbal in my support of the kind of direct relationship between the artist and consumer the web allows," Matthew said. "Publishing *Brave Men Run* independently is my way to stand with the growing number of creative people who have by-passed traditional means of media distribution."

At Podiobooks.com readers (actually they are 'listeners') can subscribe to his book, setting the pace (one episode a day, or once a week, for example).

"Some people thought it was a mistake to offer the book for free as a podcast," Matthew says. "I was confident it would serve as a marketing tool for the book – and I was right. Nearly every sale of the paperback and eBook can be traced to a podcast listener. And how many first-time authors can say their book has been experienced by tens of thousands?"

In fact, more than 30,000 people from all over the world have down-loaded *Brave Men Run* episodes. "The paperback and eBook editions are available for folks who can't wait until the end of the podcast episodes to get the whole story," says Matthew.

In April of 2006, Matthew gathered together all the episodes and released the entire book in MP3 audio book format. An MP3 CD audio book can play in most modern compact disc players and all computers; MP3 compression allowed *Brave Men Run Audio Collection* to fit on one CD instead of five in the more conventional CD audio format.

Matthew also built a website at www.bravemenrun.com, where visi-tors can obtain more information about the book.

Let's flip through Matthew's marketing mix. His **purpose** was to cre-ate art. "For me, a work of creativity is not art until it is experienced by other people. For *Brave Men Run*, success is measured by the feedback

I have received, the world-wide reach of the book, and the overwhelmingly positive response of my audience."

He spent less than $200 and happily invested hundreds of hours. He continues to devote about an hour a day to answering emails and other promoting. The money has been more than recouped. Self-publishing has also brought Matthew a loyal audience on five continents, referrals for his consulting and web hosting business, speaking engagements, and other personal and professional opportunities. (**profit** planning)

"By producing, voicing and recording the free podcast edition of *Brave Men Run* entirely by myself, I led the way for dozens of other podiobook authors, and offered them my own experiences and advice. In this way, I am giving back to the artistic community, which is one of the core elements of the DIY ethic." (**people**)

Matthew considers his **public** as a marketplace he is cultivating for his future creativity: "Consumer research, in my case, is my one-to-one, direct communication with my audience. I reply personally to every piece of correspondence, usually the same day, and am very available and open to my audience via e-mail and various messaging platforms. From this, I know that my audience embraces and encourages the new Internet merit economy, where the reader is the arbitrator of the value of the content. These people do not support – or even tolerate – content they do not like. They are vocal, and their influence is viral. Creative people who ignore the power of new media are missing out."

Promotions have been intertwined with Matthew's DIY evangelism. Matthew sent out press releases and had book signings in his local area. He is often interviewed on other people's podcasts, and speaks and appears on panels at conferences. He actively participates in online communities. "My own advocacy of citizen media, my steadfast and uncompromising adherence to the DIY ethic, and my willingness to assist others in their DIY, independent creative pursuits – in short, my personal and public behavior – builds awareness of *Brave Men Run*."

Matthew's thoughts about **price**/value reflect his creative passion:

"People respect conviction, and generally want to support it. The podcast is absolutely free, and people are encouraged to share it with others. To date, I have received more income from volunteer donations from podcast listeners than I have from royalties for the paperback edition. Again, trust your audience – they will repay you in ways both tangible and through promotion and support."

SPECIAL OR CORPORATE SALES

Publishers (and authors) dream of selling hundreds of copies directly to a large corporation who will give them to staff as an incentive or gift. Sometimes this happens, though less often than one might imagine. It appears that there needs to be a very good fit, plus a personal connection with a well-placed executive, plus considerable luck. So rare is this type of success that few large publishing houses have even one full-time staff person searching out these opportunities.

Three indie authors who have created success with special sales are Grant Hicks, Fraser Smith and Bryan Woodward. Grant pitches both his own consulting services (including motivational speaking) and his book to financial institutions and their networks of advisors. Co-written with famed marketing guru Jay Conrad Levinson, Grant's book is called *Guerrilla Marketing for Financial Advisors* [ISBN 1412003997]. When a corporation 'bites' to buy Grant's motivation service, Grant can expect to sell them lots of books – enough for everyone who will hear his presentations. What's in it for the institution? Advisors using Grant's tactics will increase their clientele of investors. Grant sold over 5,000 books, mostly through special sales, before toning down his marketing – but more about that later in this book....

Fraser Smith [*The Smith Manouevre*, ISBN 1553696417] also sells directly to his connections in the executive offices of large financial organizations. The organization stands to benefit from underwriting huge loans if its clients adopt Fraser's personal tax saving strategy. Fraser himself becomes part of this special sale when he is recruited to explain his tax-saving plan to bank employees and financial advisors.

Bryan G. Woodward knows that American doctors' clinics and Health Maintenance Organizations [HMOs] can control insurance costs by documenting 'informed consent' from patients wanting obesity surgery. By presenting each patient with Bryan's book, *A Complete Guide to Obesity Surgery: Everything You Need to Know About Weight Loss Surgery and How to Succeed* [ISBN 1552126641], the organization demonstrates commitment to providing extensive, clear information that it would be far too expensive for a doctor to recite in person. Bryan's connections as a medical professional working in the obesity field allow him access to decision-makers in many medical establishments.

If you are certain of that perfect fit and have the tenacity and the all-important connections, you may be able to make special sales into a lucrative channel.

Occasionally, with the perfect match and the persistence to keep your book in print, a special sale will happen 'out-of-the-blue.' Dr. William V. Pietsch's book, *Human BE-ing: How to Have a Creative Relationship Instead of a Power Struggle* [ISBN 1552123693], had been a best seller in the 1980s but was out-of-print for years when he decided to make a few revisions and re-publish through a POD service. Having this on-demand edition listed at various Internet search engines proved very profitable for Dr. Pietsch when a New Zealand society was able to track him down with their idea to  adapt and reprint his book. They paid royalties for a 10,000-copy print run that would be distributed as part of a social program for Maoris. Dr. Pietsch and his wife were invited Down Under to meet with the society and approve a re-designed front cover showing Maori faces.

DIRECT RESPONSE ADVERTISING DISTRIBUTION

Are you thinking about selling the book yourself – from your website or at a postal address – to customers who respond to advertising in magazines or papers, on the Internet, or in TV or radio commercials? In the publishing industry this is generally referred to as *direct response marketing* or *direct response advertising*. Using direct response marketing could be thought of as a **place** decision. It is also a choice about **paid advertising**, another of the 14-Ps. In this book, I've opted to provide the explanations and advice about direct response marketing in Chapter 9: **Paid Advertising**.

CHAPTER 4

Public(s)

Who 'buys'? Who is your 'target audience'?

What in their behavior and motivations distinguishes this group from others?

Does anyone compete with you and might benefit from your lack of success?

Every best-selling author has figured out who needs and wants the book. It is very difficult to sell to someone who doesn't both need and want your book. And it is delightfully simple to accept money from those who do – if you can make them aware of your book's existence, of course.

Your challenge in this section of the marketing mix puzzle is to figure out the market segments who both need/want your book and can be reached/persuaded in a cost-effective way. For example, 'all women who like romance novels' would be a too broadly defined group, and very expensive to reach with advertising.

'Remote control club members' was the target for *Big Jim's RC Motor Black Book* [ISBN 9781553690863] by Big Jim Greenemeyer and Hank Hagquist. Big Jim's book reveals how to get higher performance from the little remote-controlled motors used in model airplanes, boats and other hobby items. The authors contacted club executives who spread the word through emailings and printed newsletters. Articles by the authors and reviews of the book appeared in RC magazines and were posted to hobbyist websites. For months after its launch, *Big Jim's RC Motor Black Book* was one of the top selling hobby books at Amazon. com. These authors had focused on a narrowly-defined **public** to achieve top sales results.

When Lucas Akroyd wrote *1984: The Ultimate Van Halen Trivia Book* [ISBN 1552120899], he knew exactly his prospective buyer: every hard-core fan of the classic rock band. And he knew where to find them quickly and cheaply: at Van Halen fan websites. Lucas gave free copies to webmasters, in exchange for reviews and 'featured link' hyperlinks back to the book's webpage.

Lucas kept the 'news' aspect of his book alive by asking the band members to sign copies, then he interviewed them for articles he wrote and posted at those fan websites. Fan 'zines began to call him for his 'expert' opinion and insider viewpoint, with Lucas always getting in a plug for his trivia book. Because this was back in 1997, Lucas was breaking new ground, and his book was likely the highest selling on-demand title ever at that point. And all because he could accurately target the optimal **public** for this book.

Knowing his **public** (police officer trainees) told Detective Chip Morgan where to sell *Focused Interviewing* [ISBN 9781552122914]. His book teaches the best methods of criminal interrogation. He struck a deal with the US Federal Law Enforcement Training Center – where Chip sometimes lectures – selling hundreds of copies of his training manual with each successive wave of new police trainees. Remember that school bookstores typically expect a mere 15% to 25% discount off the retail price and then charge students the full retail price. Chip's royalty earnings set records in the POD world that weren't surpassed for many years.

If your market segment self-identifies by where they go or what they do, that's your clue about where, how and when to inform them. Lucas's audience go to Van Halen fan websites and read fan 'zines. Similarly, remote control enthusiasts join clubs, subscribe to RC mags, participate in dedicated newsgroups and go to hobbyist websites. Meanwhile, police trainees attend the academy. Who are your target buyers? What do they read/watch, where do they shop, what groups do they belong to? Do they attend conferences, or read newsletters? Who or what is the network 'hub' (the opinion leader or influential entity) to inform and motivate others?

With the emergence of the Internet as a field of rallying points for many niche groups, an author can think about buying specific words or phrases at search engines, so that anyone who types in 'obesity surgery' or 'civil war medicine' or 'Yukon River maps,' as examples, can be directed to your book on that topic. *(More about this form of targeted advertising later, in the chapter on Paid Advertising.)*

It is a lovely development that what was once the reason for a publishing house turning down your book – 'the audience is too narrow' – has now become the best asset a self-publisher can have. An individual author can exploit this advantage even better than a commercial publishing house, because you know your niche **public** so well.

As you are working out the marketing mix puzzle, keep an open mind because sometimes clues will take you to unexpected places. Ted and Lora Lea thought at first that the prime audience for *When I Grow Up, I Want To Be a Millionaire: A Children's Guide to Mutual Funds* [ISBN 9781552125373] would be children, or maybe

parents wanting to teach good savings and investment discipline to their children. They soon discovered that a more lucrative **public** consisted of financial advisors who needed an appropriate promotional gift for clients who had children. And later the Leas found that mutual fund companies themselves would buy copies by the hundreds to pass out to the financial advisors – who would in turn send them to clients to start their children off on a lifelong program of investing in those mutual funds. The trick is to keep asking who will benefit from your book and not limit yourself to the end user. Someone else may benefit by providing your book as a gift or promotional item.

A very practical approach is to start local, learn, then expand. 'Pick the low-hanging fruit' (sell to the easiest customers) first, then move on. Think about your network of professional and personal contacts, who will make up a great initial **public** to start that all-important word-of-mouth buzz about your new book. Though you might not think of them as your 'network,' you have family, friends, schoolmates, neighbors, fellow members of a congregation, service club, sports team or hobby group, clients, suppliers – everyone you come into contact with during a year. What if you could get them all to talk about your book to everyone in their network of contacts?

If you know 100 people and each of them tells 10 others, that's 1,000 people who quickly know about your book and why it is important. When they, in turn, talk to all their friends and contacts....

What would they tell others about your book that's so exciting? It's your **Positioning Statement**, right? We'll get to that soon.

CHAPTER 5

Price/value

What is the total cost (emotional, time, financial) for customers to buy your product or service?

What is the value a customer gains?

Is there an emotional or financial cost to the customer if they DON'T buy?

In establishing the retail price for your book, consider its importance to the reader, without overly focusing on what you are paying for print and binding. People do not buy ink on paper – they buy a *value* or *benefit*, right?

Too often, self-publishing authors will undervalue their writing. Frequently they will get confused about whether they are to be competing in price with mass-market paperbacks – even though it is economically impossible for a short-run book to be produced and sold for anywhere near the price of a million-copy pulp paperback.

Graham Wideman is one of the foremost experts on Visio, a Microsoft software program that creates charts and graphs. In 2000, he wrote a thick manual about Visio that explained the program in great depth, with far more detail than an ordinary user would need. The audience for Graham's manual consisted of software developers who create add-ons and plug-ins to Visio, and who definitely needed to know everything possible about the inner workings of Microsoft's code. Although print costs were such that he could have priced the book for as low as $20, Graham set the retail price at $49.95 for *Visio 2000 Developer's Sur-*

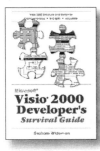

vival Guide [ISBN 155212407X] because he believed his relatively limited audience would appreciate the value of the unique information and be willing to pay accordingly.

Though self-published and produced at low cost – thanks to print-on-demand – Graham's manual had the appearance of a 'real book.' The retail price was certainly in the range of other serious technical books. The book's content quickly gained attention with developers and internally at Microsoft. That helped Graham obtain deeper insider access to forthcoming releases of Visio, and also generated some consulting work. It also set the stage for two subsequent books: *Visio 2002 Developer's Survival Pack* and *Visio 2003 Developer's Survival Pack.*

In the initial period after each of the later books was released, bulk orders totalling over 1,000 copies were received from software companies whose developers urgently needed the new technical content. By picking a high retail price, Graham earned thousands of dollars more in margin and royalties than if he'd under-priced it. So not only did the $49.95 price tag give the book credibility, it also meant Graham wasn't leaving money on the table.

Of course, **price** isn't only about money. Sometimes a relatively small change to your book can dramatically affect the perceived value in the mind of a potential buyer. What about having a snappy endorsement ('Thoroughly captivating!' 'Couldn't put it down!' 'Brilliant first novel!') on the cover? That might break down a major psychological barrier about buying a book by a novice author at any price. Paying $15 for an unendorsed book may be harder to do than paying $25 for a 'sure thing' endorsed by a celebrity.

If you think a celebrity endorsement might help your book's value proposition, www.celebritycontactpage.com is a website for contact information about 63,000 actors and other famous people. It costs $9.99 to join for a week and do unlimited researching. The downside is that few celebrities respond to emails and other unsolicited communications. Nonetheless, the website is a place to start, and provides great opportunities for daydreaming.

If your non-fiction book's value is focused on specialized information, could you offer a free subscription to weekly reports? For a novel, how about promising an emailed version of the sequel when that is ready?

Have you thought about the difference a guarantee can make? How about coupons to redeem for services? Some authors find those ideas cheesy and potentially devaluing to their book. Others writing business books, for example, might feel that such offers will enhance the price-value proposition with their target audience.

For 60 years, Henry Cohen advised companies and nonprofits on how to use direct mail advertising to sell their products and services to millions of people. He was responsible (like it or not) for much of the junk mail you may have received in your lifetime. True to form, Henry wrote 'Find out how to win a FABULOUS prize!' in blue ink on the cover of his self-published memoir,  *I Sent You A Letter... Did You Reply? True Tales of a Junk Mail Whiz* [ISBN 1553690893]. How can a reader win that prize? You'll have to buy and read Henry's book to find out!

When you set the retail price for your book, you may have the option, depending on which publishing service you are using, to pick prices in multiple currencies: US dollars, Canadian dollars, British pounds sterling and euro, for example. Regardless of the price you initially pick in each international currency, they won't always be exact conversions later since the currencies constantly fluctuate in value compared to each other.

Does $19.99 or $19.95 seem significantly more affordable to you than $20.00? Most retailers apparently believe this holds true for the majority of their customers and products. However, Tom Reilly, our authority on all things Irish, contends that a price of 13.99 euro seems very tacky for a book – it would project a more confident, sophisticated and 'valuable' air at an even 14.00 euro, he advises.

Once you set the retail price(s), it is important that you stick to your price in each currency. A price change causes a long chain of grief and confusion within the book trade because everyone must change their information (and sticker over old pricing) and risk being stuck with overpriced stock if the price goes down. This inertia and resistance means that it is not practical to experiment frivolously with pricing once the book is released. You're better off revising content and other aspects of your marketing mix, and leaving price change as a last resort.

CHAPTER 6

Positioning

What makes what you provide or the way you provide it unique (i.e. what is the USP = unique sales proposition)?

What is the best concise argument (the key messages) you can make for your product or service?

Assess your identity (how you try to project yourself and your book) and your image (how others actually perceive you) – is there a gap? To be successful, how must you and your book be perceived?

What is your branding? How are you packaging your product/service?

Why would anyone want (and need!) to buy your book? Figure out the very best reasons why your book will help them to transform their lives. Then work on condensing that argument into one or two sentences. THIS is your **positioning** statement.

You could also call it your 'elevator pitch' since you must be able to deliver it in the time it takes an elevator to rise a few floors – imagining you are on an elevator and this is your only opportunity to pitch your book to Oprah Winfrey herself.

You will end up presenting this concise pitch thousands of times:

- to each journalist, explaining why they simply *must* review your book,
- to radio and TV producers, convincing them why their audience *must* learn about your book,
- to potential readers as they ask you in person – as they will by the hundreds – 'What's your book about?' even though they are really asking, 'What's in it for me and why should I buy it?'
- to bookstore managers, convincing them to stock your book,
- to your audience at book signings, readings, launch event and during interviews, and
- maybe even to a celebrity in an elevator!

People will only remember at most two or three 'facts' from any conversation/news release/interview, so you must figure out your best points to be delivered at the start of the interaction, and repeated at the end. Keep stating your positioning statement again and again and again. In marketing, repetition is deemed essential – consistency and continuity will build a brand identity.

Jay Levinson, writing in *Guerrilla Marketing for Writers* [ISBN 9780898799835], advises that, "You must make potential readers confident in you. Consistency creates familiarity, familiarity builds confidence, and confidence is the most important factor in determining what makes consumers buy. It's more important than quality, selection, price and service."

Consider writing out a slightly different positioning statement for each market segment that you'll be pursuing.

Author Larry Checco is a branding expert who wrote *Branding for*

Success: A Roadmap for Raising the Visibility and Value of Your Non-profit Organization [ISBN 9781412052498]. Here's Larry's positioning statement for his firm: "Checco Communications is a consulting firm that specializes in branding. We help organizations clearly define who they are, what they do, how they do it – and why anyone should care enough to support them."

See how his book's elevator pitch is similar: "In *Branding for Success*, Larry Checco debunks the notion that branding is the sole domain of large, well-funded corporations that can afford multimillion-dollar advertising budgets and celebrity endorsements. You, too, through efficient and cost-effective means, can raise the visibility and value – namely, the brand – of your organization in powerful and meaningful ways.

"There is nothing in this book that is beyond the reach of any organization, regardless of size or financial resources. The book's two primary objectives are: (1) to make the case for branding and its importance to the sustainability – and perhaps even the survivability – of your organization; and (2) to make the fundamental principles of good branding accessible to everyone.

"In short, *Branding for Success* will help you answer the questions: Who are we? What do we do? How do we do it? And why should anyone care enough to support us?"

Larry wanted *Branding for Success* to be a very approachable one-hour read, leaving people saying, "This is something I can do." The book's **purpose** is to raise the visibility of Larry's personal and corporate brand, and to help nonprofits.

Larry believes that *everything* you do and say becomes part of your brand – that branding is essentially your organization's DNA. When you, as an author, are creating a positioning statement, it will be effective at convincing the potential buyer only if it rings true with everything you are doing. Therefore you can see how **positioning** (branding) acts to determine which marketing activities are appropriate to undertake.

Here's some of what Larry has done to build his own brand:

- created a company website (www.checcocomm.net) where he can explain about branding and his firm's mission and capabilities,
- added a webpage to take book orders (and obtain email addresses for following up to promote his firm's work),
- ensured the book is available at Amazon.com and other retailers by publishing through a POD publishing service,
- written a short quarterly newsletter that is emailed to all his contacts and prospects, and is quoted in the newsletters of many huge associations for nonprofits,
- given away hundreds of copies to CEOs of nonprofits who may become future clients,
- sold the book at his speaking engagements at conferences, and
- taught web seminars ('webinars') and been interviewed on 'De-Mystifying Nonprofits' at www.GlobalTalkRadio.com.

Larry didn't spend a penny on advertising. He didn't need to and doing so wouldn't be consistent with his own branding message to nonprofits about being efficient and taking advantage of the resources they already have.

Did Larry succeed? Judging by his **purpose**, yes. *Branding for Success* sold almost a thousand copies in less than a year, more than repaying all of Larry's investment. His personal profile has been raised and his firm has experienced an increase in consulting work helping nonprofits.

Creating a positioning statement is similar to writing a very compelling short story. You want your message to be memorable – to retailers, potential buyers, their friends and anyone else. A thought-provoking book on creating a great positioning statement is *Made to Stick: Why Some Ideas Survive and Others Die* by Chip and Dan Heath [ISBN 9781400064281].

CHAPTER 7

Partnerships

*Who can help in a mutually-beneficial (synergistic)
relationship? Can you find a way to create a more
valuable product offering or package by selling your
product in combination with that of a partnering
company?*

*Who shares your space without mutual benefit?
Can something be done to enlist them in
mutually-beneficial marketing?*

Although 'everyone needs to earn a living' seems like a cliché, that thought does basically explain why **partnerships** are so effective for indie authors. If you can pick out someone who will benefit from your book's success, then you can have a strongly self-motivated ally on your team.

Similarly, if there are individuals or groups who are threatened by your potential for book sales, it is wise to figure this out early on, and plan accordingly. You might be able to use some business ju-jitsu to turn their thinking around to your and their mutual benefit.

Let's consider how partnerships played a key role in Ken Roueche's profitable experience as the indie author of *A Fairfield History* [ISBN 1412060354]. Here's Ken's account, with my notations about Ps in square brackets:

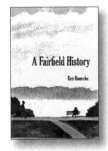

"About six years ago I started researching the history of my Victoria neighborhood, Fairfield. I thought I would like to test my skills as a writer and satisfy a curiosity about this beautiful place. *[purpose]*

"While pulling the writing together, I was also thinking about publishing. Some of my advisers were initially keen to see me use a traditional publisher, "…let them take all the risks and pay you royalties." However, I determined that this book was not likely to be a big seller beyond Fairfield and therefore probably not of interest to publishers, who are looking for sales in the thousands, not just a few hundred. I was also advised that publishers invariably ask authors to help develop a marketing strategy. What?! I was going to sell this book to the 14,000 people who live in Fairfield, full stop. More fundamentally, I had also determined that I could probably finance the project myself, and maybe not lose too much money. *[calculating **profits**]*

"Covers of a book are perhaps the most important pages. The art work was created by Robert Amos, a well-known Victoria artist and resident of Fairfield. When I approached Robert about the project, I told him I couldn't afford to pay to commission original art work. His response was, "Don't worry, I'm in. Pay me an honorarium if you are successful, which you will be." *[partnership]*

"The total cost to prepare the book for print, collect photos, pay archival royalties, prepare a custom-made map of the neighborhood and print 250 copies was around $6,000. *[calculating **profits**]*

"Meanwhile, I had been doing a little research on book marketing. I spoke to booksellers in Victoria and quickly recognized that this was not a route to profitability, at least not for a small time author/publisher. At this point I had also determined that the pricing needed to be simple.

I surveyed the prices of similar books in local bookstores. This led me to the 'no change, no taxes, $20 gets you a copy of my book' strategy. I hoped that this would help reduce the barriers to a sale. *[price]*

"Several weeks prior to the launch, an excerpt from my book titled *The Great Government House Fire* was printed in the Sunday edition of the *Times-Colonist*. They even paid me for it! *[publicity; partnership]*

"During week two, I had my first media interview on CBC Radio Victoria. At this point, I was also contacted by Cathy Sorensen, who had just opened a bookstore in the neighborhood, Sorensen Books at 1027 Cook Street. Cathy saw my book as a vehicle to help establish her presence in Fairfield. I advised her that paying regular bookseller commissions was going to make it very difficult for me to break-even. (Break-even, hell, I was just hoping to lose as little money as possible.) With gross revenues on about 330 books I could just about get my money back; but with 40% commissions to bookstores I would need to sell hundreds more books. We were able to work out a business strategy that helped ensure the financial viability of my project and make *A Fairfield History* the top selling book for Sorensen Books in their first year of operation. The book is available exclusively at Sorensen Books. *[partnership; place]*

"On day fifteen I appeared on the Susan Woods Show on C-FAX Radio's *Remember When* and two days later I appeared on the CH-TV Noon Hour Program with Murray Langdon. Several days earlier, while out trolling for customers, I had met Murray at the Beagle Pub in Fairfield. I approached him with my usual subtlety: "Hey, aren't you that TV guy? You need one of my books." Remember: *never leave home without the book!* His response: "…looks great, we need you on our show." *[partnership; publicity]*

"During the twenty-minute interview I was able to answer a number of phone-in questions and announce a book signing for the coming Friday at Sorensen Books. Robert Amos was also in attendance and signed the cover art. *[publicity; partnerships]*

"Break-even was reached on August 19 (day 33) with 333 books sold.

"I have always enjoyed walking and soon discovered that walking around was a great way to sell my book. The $20 selling price was really reducing the barriers on street sales. It was also apparent that many people were interested in my book but not prepared, or able, to make an impulse purchase. A hand-out was required. I determined that the most cost-effective hand-out would be a copy of the customized map of Fairfield that appears in the book, along with a write-up on the back about the book and where to buy it. This seemed to work very well. Now my question was: "Would you like one of my historic maps of Fairfield?" A significant number took my map, some inquired about the reason for the map, some asked to see the book and not infrequently a sale was made. *[personal sales; sales promotion (sample)]*

"Encounters on my walks with a class of nine-years-olds, a room full of 80-year-olds, visitors from Sacramento and San Antonio, and a Jamaican cricketer all added to a very special adventure which seemed to be delivering customers to Sorensen Books. *[partnership]*

"By Labour Day, bookstore sales reached 110 and continued to build through to the Christmas season, approaching 250 by year end. *Boulevard Magazine* also gave the book a recommendation, one of three, in their Christmas issue. Total sales for 2005 hit 585.

"The book was featured in the January issue of *Senior Living Magazine* and in the first issue of the *Moss Rocks Review*. *[publicity]*

"Sales to date are 705. I am not certain if my modest success could be repeated. I may have simply lucked into a unique combination of circumstances:

- a book-hungry niche audience *[public]* that wanted this book *[product]*
- a small geographically-defined market that readily suited guerrilla marketing *[place; personal sales]*, and

- strong support from a neighborhood artist, a neighborhood bookstore and the local media. *[partnerships; publicity]*

"The bottom line: it was gratifying to experience the strong response from my neighbors to *A Fairfield History*.

"In recognition of the unique circumstances that allowed for the success of my book, I have declared, frequently and loudly, that I will be a one-book wonder. However, with a few dollars in my jeans from this surprising success (remember the original business plan was to lose as little money as possible), I went searching for another history project, this time with others hopefully producing the majority of the content. That project, to create and sell books about small Jamaican towns, has begun and I hope will, someday, lead to great things.

"Your comments and feedback are welcomed.

"– Ken Roueche kroueche@shaw.ca October 11, 2006"

Certainly Ken was clever to identify who in the community would make great **partners**. The bookstore owner needed a way to introduce her new store to the locals, so having an exclusive on bookstore sales of Ken's book worked well. Although Cathy received a smaller margin than is standard, overall this was inexpensive marketing for her.

Artist Robert Amos traded artwork for a future honorarium and publicity. Ken got a handsome cover.

The local media always need stories, and Ken was a source of intriguing anecdotes about Fairfield's past. In one case, Ken even got paid for providing an excerpt to the newspaper. For Ken it was publicity; for the *Times-Colonist* it was content. That's a good **partnership** to cultivate.

Fraser Smith retired in 2002 with a bee in his bonnet. Not a literal bumblebee, but a grand injustice was really bugging him. During his lengthy and successful career as a financial planner and tax specialist, Fraser had seen how US homeowners could legally deduct the interest component of their mortgage payments from their income taxes, yet

Canadians weren't allowed to do the same by their government's regulations. Meanwhile he saw that many of Canada's wealthier citizens, with the assistance of top tax accountants and lawyers, were using clever means to deduct the interest on their house mortgage loans. Because of complexity and cost, these kinds of practices were not available to Canadians of average means – the other 90% of the population.

Fraser also noted that too many Canadians were waiting until their mortgages were paid off before they started to build an investment portfolio, missing out on years of compounding interest, and putting themselves in the position of being 'house rich and cash poor in retirement.'

After studying Canada's tax rules extensively, and working closely with the highly-regarded VanCity Credit Union, Fraser developed a simple and powerful strategy that extends the tax advantages of the wealthy to Canadians of average means in an affordable, elegant and legal way.

Fraser explained what he called 'The Smith Manoeuvre' in a self-published book of the same name [ISBN 0973295201].

Merely having a book available wasn't going to spread the word and start the country-wide tax-saving revolution that Fraser wanted. His solution: **partnerships**.

Fraser used his extensive contacts in the financial community to ally with several financial institutions. Fraser's manoeuvre involves taking out a new loan and investing in various securities – which is great news for banks and credit unions eager to underwrite the loans, for financial planners who would help the homeowner invest tax refunds, and for mutual funds who would be the recipients of the investment dollars.

Several financial institutions hired Fraser to teach the technique to their financial planners. On his website at www.smithman.net, Fraser soon listed almost 500 planners across Canada who were promoting this tax-saving technique to their clients.

Through **partnerships**, Fraser is seeing his dream come true –

Canadian families making their mortgages tax-deductible, and increasing their net worth significantly. In a few years, his book sold 30,000 copies and he'll soon launch a second book on do-it-yourself pension plans.

Not one to rest on his laurels, Fraser plans to **partner** with two other respected businessmen to set up a national firm called the Smith Manoeuvre Financial Corporation. SMFC has the goal of nationalizing the Smith Manoeuvre via the mortgage brokerage channel. Their plans include offering the Smith Manoeuvre Mortgage, the Smith Manoeuvre Personal Pension Fund and the Smith Manoeuvre Secured Investment Lending program. To top it off they intend to have a fleet of financial planners (more **partners**!) to offer planning services as well.

If you have a book that others could rally around, think about fostering **partnerships**.

Remember the two women who wrote *Muffins: A Cookbook*? Joan and Marilyn partnered with cookware manufacturer Ecco to offer a single purchase item to housewives: a muffin pan and their muffin cookbook were shrink-wrapped together and offered at a price slightly less than buying each item separately. From the consumer's point of view, the cookbook was useless if that consumer didn't already have a muffin pan, and the pan wasn't usable without recipes. Through a **partnership**, the combined products took on extra value. The authors also benefited from all the extra sales venues (**places**) that Ecco reached – hardware and cookery stores.

WHAT ABOUT POTENTIALLY ADVERSE RELATIONSHIPS?

When Fraser Smith first began helping average Canadians beat the taxman, he was seen by some financial planners and institutions as a competitor and a threat to their own business. To any competitor, Smith's methods were controversial and might draw away clients. But the very planners who had the most to lose could also be those with the most to gain – it was all in perceptions. So, rather than keeping the strategy exclusively for his own use, Fraser made a conscious decision to share the knowledge with as many people as possible – by explaining it in his book and by partnering with all planners and institutions. Within three years, he had converted thousands of potential adversaries (pit bulls) into enthusiastic partners (puppies). Over 500 planners were listed on his website as local resources for any homeowners buying the book.

When you perceive of someone or some group as a potential adversary, look for a way to invert the perception and enlist them as partners.

CHAPTER 8

Promotional mix – personal sales

To whom will you be personally communicating and how?

What are the key messages?

What specific personal sales ideas will you implement?

[The following story borrows heavily from a review by Alan Twigg of *Never Chop Your Rope* by the late Joe Garner, which appeared in BC BookWorld, Autumn 1988. Used by permission. See www.abcbookworld.com. *Thanks, Alan!*]

In my home province of British Columbia, the name Joe Garner is almost synonymous with self-publishing – and with personal book sales success. Joe was a retired logger and bush pilot who simply loved to promote his books. His first book, a memoir called *Never Fly Over an Eagle's Nest* was reprinted 25 times between 1980 and 1998. Joe was famous for driving his van around the country to persuade bookstore and café owners to stock his books. He thought nothing of riding the BC ferries (for free because he was a senior and it was a weekday) all day to buttonhole fellow passengers. He'd tell a story so engaging that a crowd would gather – and he'd soon be exchanging books for cash.

Joe wrote a series of books that gave his story-telling personal sales performances more options: *Never a Time to Trust, Never Chop Your Rope, Never Under the Table,* and *Never Forget the Good Times.*

"The big thing about publishing," said logger and author Joe Gamer, 79, "is promotion. You can't be a dreamer. You have to get out there and talk to people. I just came back from Cassiar and the Alaska Highway and sold out all the books I had. When I go north on a trip I sometimes sell as many books in a day as some people sell in a lifetime."

Garner was a firm believer in the self-publishing process. "It is more profitable than trying to exist on royalties," he said, "You do have control. And if you have enough common sense you can profit from your own hard work.

"We have traveled across Canada twice in our motor home, calling on book outlets, the news media and book review people. We get repeat orders from over 70 per cent of these contacts. But the most gratifying thing about such trips is the people you meet."

ARE THEY BOOK SIGNING OR EVENTS?

My thanks to Marcelo Beilin for his suggestions in this next section.

As author of *How to Reinvent Yourself: Inspiring Strategies for Personal Renewal* [ISBN 1412061482], Marcelo Beilin conducted over 40 author events at big-box chain bookstores, with book sales ranging anywhere from 25 to over 100 books per event. To publicize these events, he arranged to be featured on more than 50 media outlets, ranging from local radio and print to national newspapers, radio and TV in both the US and Canada. Although this was a part-time endeavor, he achieved book sales of over 2,000 copies within two years, selling out his initial print run. More success: a Mexican publisher bought Spanish-language rights to the book.

We need to demystify book signings and turn them into a true book-selling opportunity. Why use the word demystify? Because there is a myth among authors that book signings are a great way to sell books. Truth be told, book signings may do something for our egos, but they don't really do much for book sales. The reason for this is, unless you are an already-famous author or a media celebrity, customers will likely perceive you as a stranger sitting at a table, pen in hand, with a pile of books at your side, looking rather uncomfortable and maybe a bit forlorn. Generally people will avoid you, since few people buy books out of pity.

Does that sound depressing? Well, you can do better. Please read on....

The blunt truth is that – according to an executive at Barnes & Noble – on average, a typical book signing will create sales of only FOUR copies! By contrast, at *events*, authors can sell dozens, even hundreds of copies.

Selling is about creating an emotional connection between a customer and a product or service. Buying books is no different, except that in this case, the emotional connection has to be made between you and your book's content, and the individual customer. In order for people to buy a new book from an unknown author, they need to get to know the author first. You have to provide them with the opportunity to meet you and to connect with you and your book. You need to turn an otherwise dull book signing into an exciting event that energizes people into buying copies of your book. Have them so enthused they won't leave the store unless they get your autograph first!

How do you turn a book signing into a book-selling event? The answer depends on what type of book you are trying to sell. If yours is a how-to book, then you may create a workshop where you can teach potential buyers a few of the tricks of the trade that you have accumulated over the years. Give them a taste of your knowledge or expertise, and do not divulge all your secrets. The goal of these events is to always leave your potential customers wanting more – a thirst that can naturally be quenched by purchasing your book.

Remember that your aim is to create an emotional connection with your audience. How does one go about doing this, you wonder? The answer is quite simple: be yourself and do not try to be something you are not. Authenticity is one of the best means for engaging with an audience. Be your best self and share your message with enthusiasm. Answer your audience's questions with honesty and, above all, don't try to 'hard-sell' them your book. Focus on the benefits of the information in it instead. People, for the most part, don't like to be badgered. They just want the opportunity to connect with your message in a way that is meaningful to them. If this connection is achieved in the course of your event, the sale will be a natural extension of this process.

If your message resonates with your audience, they'll be lining up to buy your book and talk to you. Marcelo held bookstore events where a hundred people would come to see him talk and as many books would be sold by the end of the evening. Even more books would be sold in the week following the event as word-of-mouth recommendations spread.

If your book is a novel, memoir or a poetry book, one option is to structure your event as an author reading plus some teaching. If this is the format you choose to use, keep in mind that in order to connect with your audience, you will have to do more than just read. You will have to perform. If you are reading a novel, you'll want to use a different tone of voice to dramatize each of the characters. And, you want to really act it out to give your audience an experience, and not be just a talking head.

Consider telling stories interspersed with passages from your book. For example, if your book is a memoir, you may want to tell interesting stories about your life, instead of reading word-for-word from your book. People love to hear real-life stories. By *telling* rather than *reading* your stories, it is more likely that your natural humor and warmth will come out and keep the audience engaged.

If you have a poetry book, you can share with your audience what it was that inspired you to write a specific poem. Before you read each poem, give them the context and background in which your poem came to life. Again, people love to hear stories. Also, if your reading has been inspired by or based on a specific part of the country, you can educate your audience about interesting aspects of this region as a way of engaging them before you do your reading. For example, if some of your poems were inspired by a trip to India, promote that fact on your flyers and show a few slides of your trip when doing the reading. You could be surprised how many people from that region come simply to see your pictures, and end up buying a copy of your book.

How else could you stage a poetry event? How about a presentation of 'The Four Golden Steps to Writing Publishable Poetry'? Or maybe a speed poetry writing demonstration in which the audience picks a topic? Or offer free 5-minute critiques (gentle ones) to aspiring poets?

Now that you have created an exciting event for your audience, the next thing to do is to find a good venue for your event. The most cost-effective venue for author events is, quite logically, bookstores. Libraries may allow you to do author events, but may not allow you to sell your books there. Go to local bookstores and ask to talk to the store manager (or the marketing manager, in the case of chain stores). Tell them what your plans are for your author event, and make sure you bring a sample copy of your book to leave behind.

If you are dealing with large bookstore chains, they may ask you to put together an event proposal. If this is the case, don't panic. All they want to know is that you are a legitimate author. What you have to do is write out what your book is about, the nature of your event (seminar, reading, workshop, etc.) and more importantly, what are you going to do specifically to promote your event. This last point is crucial because it shows the manager that you are serious about selling your book and that you are capable of bringing people into the store (which could generate ancillary sales for the bookstore).

You must promote your event so as many people as possible find out about it. Marcelo found that his most popular events followed an appearance on a local radio talk show, or an article about his book appearing in community newspapers. Eventually, he worked his way up to mainstream radio and national TV, but not before he had created significant exposure through the local community-based outlets. The main point to remember here is timing. Depending on the size and popularity of the bookstore, you may have to book your event weeks and sometimes months in advance in order to get into the queue. Once you have some dates nailed down, immediately begin the media promotion campaign.

Incidentally, you don't have to restrict yourself just to media. Make sure you send invitations to absolutely everyone you know, even if you don't know them well – because you never know who will buy your book and who won't. In addition, post fliers in local libraries, coffee shops, restaurants and bars, always making sure you ask permission first. Look for any public bulletin board within a reasonable radius of the event location.

Another great tool to promote free events is to send a one- or two-line synopsis of the event with the date, time and location to the event listing section of newspapers and entertainment magazines in your area. This is a free public service in most publications! In order to submit your blurb, simply collect a copy of the papers and magazines in which you would like to be listed, look for their fax number in the section showing their contact information, and fax in your request. You'll be surprised how many of them will publish your event listing, and how many people will read this. A reporter may even call you up for more details and create an article for the Lifestyle section.

The key here is to inform as many people as possible about your event, and to do so in the most cost-effective way. Most new authors get more results working on a shoestring budget than through paid services, such as display advertising. Of course, there are always exceptions. For instance, sometimes the large chain stores will offer cooperative advertising opportunities to authors who conduct events at their book-stores, in order to help in the promotion. Ask the marketing manager of your local chain store for details on how you and the bookstore could split the cost of a co-op ad. These ads will typically cost you a few hundred dollars.

So, don't do a plain-old book signing. Instead, create a personal sales event full of energy and excitement that will allow your audience the opportunity to connect with you and your message. Book sales success will then be a natural outcome.

CHAPTER 9

Promotional mix – paid advertising

*To whom will you be communicating through paid ads and
in which newspapers, magazines or other media?*

What are the key messages?

*What specific advertising will you purchase? How will you
monitor the results?*

W ill advertising work for you and your book? Maybe – it depends on how and where you advertise. In this section I'll give
you some explanations and advice to improve your chances.

Let's quickly get past the daydream of buying a $20,000 ad in a
glossy upscale magazine and then receiving $100,000 in royalties or di-
rect sales margin soon afterward. If the marketplace functioned that way,
everyone would quit his or her day jobs and become a millionaire author
like you. Even the largest publishing houses are quite tight with spending on *display advertising* – that's the term for any ad that isn't in the
classified section – because display ads really don't work all that well
for book sales even when promoting a likely bestseller by a politician or
other (in-)famous celebrity.

Similarly, brand-building ads for books on TV and radio are rare because publishers don't experience sufficient extra sales to pay for the high costs of production and broadcast time.

It may do your ego wonders to see your name and book's cover in the *New York Times Review of Books* section, but if you have some way of measuring sales impact, you could be left wondering if there was *any* benefit at all. Therefore, unless your **purpose** indicates that being seen in upscale places is essential and you have very deep pockets to underwrite your ego, you may wish to give general display advertising a pass.

But hold on – there are some potentially lucrative approaches to advertising, and these are variations of what is called **direct response advertising**. The key is very selective targeting and meticulous measuring of results.

When I was building Trafford Publishing, we used direct response advertising in print media (mostly magazines) and on the Internet (mostly the tiny text-only ads shown on search engines and other webpages) to attract and persuade more than 10,000 authors from around the globe to publish their books through us. We were being as targeted as possible and somewhat obsessive about measuring results – in order to continually lower the cost of attracting a new author by improving the ads and the choices of magazines and web services.

Until quite recently – the early 2000s was the turning point – the most common direct response scenarios were ads placed in magazines and other periodicals, or letters and flyers delivered to homes. The ads or letters directed the reader to send an order with a check or money order through the mail – hence the older term *mail order advertising*. Although much modern direct response advertising is now done on the Internet, and the responses come via email or toll-free phone rather than snail mail, the underlying principles remain the same.

What are your options as an author wanting to try direct response advertising? Consider these tactics, which account for selling billions of dollars worth of merchandise of all kinds every year:

- magazine and newspaper mail-order ads (think smaller display and classified ads – a practical option for some non-fiction authors),
- lengthy TV commercials (called infomercials – probably too complicated and expensive for most books),
- radio spots (ads urging you to call a 1-800 number right away – again, this is a complicated and expensive business to get into, especially if you only have one book),
- letters to the home or office (direct mail or 'junk mail' – a possibility if you have a very targeted list of names and addresses),
- Internet advertising (worth considering for non-fiction books),
- targeted emails (an option for some authors), and
- bulk emailing (called *spam*, this is not recommended).

Unfortunately, it is unlikely you can make direct response advertising profitable for poetry or fiction. For non-fiction authors, the mail-order ads and Internet advertising are likely to be the most viable direct advertising channels.

Here's some excellent news: if you can find a wide-circulation, direct response advertising vehicle that produces sales for your book in a cost-effective manner, you may have discovered a lever that you can pull to generate sales and profits at your discretion, almost forever. And you can then create other, similar levers.

By cost-effective, we mean that you are bringing in enough revenues on these sales to more than cover all your ad costs and your printing, shipping and other overheads.

More excellent news: direct response sales won't harm bookstore sales. Instead, the ads will be building general awareness of your book. Some impact will come directly to you as orders that you can measure, while the advertising will also boost your other sales channels – although this latter impact will be difficult to quantify.

Here are the steps to determine whether there is a viable direct response advertising vehicle for your book:

Step 1: Identify your target audience of readers. You've done this already – this is your **public**. Who are they? What motivates them? What are their reading and web-surfing habits?

Step 2: Identify the print publications and Internet search terms you will try. Where does your public go: which magazines do they read and which words would they enter at Google or another search site?

Step 3: Create the ad copy to attract the right people. Then create the rest of the pitch that will motivate them to buy your book (this is your **positioning**).

Step 4: Run some test insertions with *keys* so you can know from where your traffic of buyers is coming. Any ad that you insert *must* have a built-in way for you to track its results. This is typically done by having a unique codeword or promotional number in the ad – this is called the *key*. For example, the buyer may be told to ask for extension 3261 when calling. You'll know that corresponds to the June issue of a specific magazine, because there really is no extension 3261. Similarly mail will arrive addressed c/o Dept. 3261.

Step 5: Meticulously record every sale and its key.

Step 6: Analyze the results so you can continue with the ad designs and places that are profitable (and possibly increase the frequency), and drop those that don't deliver good results.

Step 7: Test new ads and places against your best producers (your *control*), investing your profits to steadily increase the number of places and the results.

FINDING PUBLICATIONS AND PAYING THE RIGHT PRICE

For Step 2, when checking out periodicals, a good sign is the number of other companies running direct response ads. Advertisers won't repeat ads in publications that have generally poor response. If possible, discover and test wherever a direct competitor is having success.

In North America, to look up costs and circulation for periodicals, check out Standard Rate and Data Service – www.srds.com. Some larger business libraries subscribe to SR&D's huge printed directories, or will have a subscription to the online database. If you don't have any luck at a library, contact an ad agency to beg or borrow an older copy of their consumer directory. Other regions of the world will have their own advertising directories that you can learn about by searching on Google for 'magazine advertising rates.'

Another option is to visit any large newstand and buy copies of magazines and news publications that cater to your intended audience and that have a lot of mail order advertising in them. Contact those publications and request their media kit, the package of information and rates provided free to advertisers.

As a general rule, you want to pick a magazine that has a low cost per reader. This is measured as CPM, cost per thousand readers. You might want to be aware that CPM is not the cost per thousand *impressions* (i.e. number of copies printed and circulated), but is instead the cost per thousand *estimated readers* (i.e. it is based on an expectation that there will be 3 or 4 readers of each copy in circulation). Of course, you want to favor a magazine whose readers will be in your specific target audience.

Although it might seem uncomfortable to you, negotiating the ad price at a magazine is common and no one will be surprised or offended. After all, the goal on both sides is for you to be able to advertise repeatedly and *profitably* – forever.

Most magazines offer discounts of 10% to 25% off the regular advertising rates to mail order advertisers – but you must ask for the discount. With persistence and by committing to six or more consecutive insertions, you may be able to get down to half of the posted one-insertion price.

Ad space obviously has a very limited shelf life – the publisher must sell the space before the magazine goes to press or will not receive any money at all. That means you can often negotiate significantly lower rates for last-minute 'remnant' space (often half-price or less). You have nothing to lose by asking for a lower rate, or for remnants, especially when you are testing a new ad or publication.

Many publications will offer special rates to get you to test with them. Later you may be able to persuade them to continue with the test rate by explaining that "based on our results, we can't afford to pay any more than $X."

Internet advertising is generally measured in cost-per-click (CPC), not cost per thousand readers. A click happens when someone actually clicks on the ad to go through to your website. We'll explain more about Internet advertising later in this chapter.

Writing copy that sells

There is a real art to creating direct response ads that work. If you are seriously committing to advertising your book, it could be prudent to hire a professional copywriter to develop your first test ads. You can also learn a lot by reading through any of these classics:

- *Ogilvie on Advertising* by David Ogilvy [ISBN 039472903X]
- *Successful Direct Marketing Methods* by Bob Stone & Ron Jacobs [ISBN 9780658001451]
- *Direct Marketing Strategies and Tactics: Unleash the Power of Direct Marketing* by Herschell Lewis [ISBN 9780850132205]
- *Tested Advertising Methods, 5th Edition* by John Caples and Fred Hahn [ISBN 9780130957016]

A text-intensive direct response ad will take this well-recognized pattern:

- the headline, subhead and any photo or illustration will

    attract the attention of the right readers (highlighting a problem, such as being unattractively overweight) and promise a benefit (such as easily becoming thin and desirable)

- the introductory text will bluntly describe the reader's problem, then declare a solution is available (i.e. your diet secrets)
- next the problem is discussed in dramatic detail, followed by an elaboration on the solution with emphasis on building credibility (e.g., you have lost 150 pounds yourself, the special ingredient is based on NASA scientific discoveries, the plan has been successfully used by hundreds of people, doctors have endorsed it...)
- longer ad copy generally produces better results than shorter copy ("The more you say, the more you sell.")
- next you need to ask bluntly for the sale, and give a reason for urgency ("20% off but only if you buy today!")
- offer a guarantee
- there will be captions and a postscript that repeat and reinforce the key messages.

If you are placing Internet search ads – through Google's AdWords or Yahoo! – you will be testing twenty-word ads that are essentially the headline and subhead that will draw someone to a special webpage (called a landing page) where the above classic direct response pattern will be presented.

TRACKING AND ANALYZING RESULTS USING THE 'KEYS'

As mentioned previously, any ad that you insert *must* have a way for you to track its results. Typically, this is done by having a unique keyed code in the ad. A respondent to a magazine ad would call and ask for extension #1043 or department 1043 or to enter promo code 1043. By tracking all orders and inquiries by the ad key, you will be able to determine your cost per order. Cost-per-order is the ultimate determination of the success of that particular ad insertion.

To track Internet response, you will need to have multiple *landing pages* at your website, one for each ad key, so a click-through will go to, for example, www.mybooktitle.com/5MF for the online ad with tracking key 5MF.

The beauty of using the Internet is that you can randomly test the impact of changing even a few words, and see the impact within only a few hours. A similar random test of a magazine print ad requires a *split run* that is expensive and will take months to show results. A split run is having two versions of an ad appearing randomly in the same position on the same page within copies of a single issue. This is possible because magazine pages are printed in huge sheets that are then folded into the final size. Generally a very wide press is used and two nearly-identical versions of the magazine are printed side-by-side on the roll of paper. The only difference between versions is your ads (and other split-run ads). Your two ads will have different text and/or graphics and different tracking keys, right? The finished magazines coming off the end of the press are co-mingled before being distributed to subscribers and stores, creating a perfectly random test.

You must have real patience for print advertising because the turnaround time for each test is several months if you are using monthly publications. You can shorten the turnaround time by testing classified ads in daily or weekly publications, but unfortunately those results may not be an accurate predictor of the results you would achieve by advertising in monthly or quarterly publications.

Internet ads don't have any delay between 'publication date' (when they are shown) and response (click-throughs), producing all their enquiries immediately. By comparison, magazines tend to be read and passed along, then put aside for later re-reading. Inquiries and sales may arrive as much as 10 years after your ad was published in a monthly magazine. Nonetheless, it is a fairly safe assumption that about half of your orders and inquiries will arrive within 30 days of publication and the remainder will trickle in over the following months and years. Ads in dailies or weeklies produce a faster (but often weaker) response with a much shorter 'tail.'

A small direct response advertising campaign may be a relatively inexpensive way to test and discover how to increase the sales of your book explosively, *but only if* you can create an ad that generates demand for your book and you can identify publications and search terms that are cost-efficient. By repeating proven ads and dropping any under-performing publications, you can grow your sales consistently and profitably.

MORE ABOUT INTERNET ADVERTISING

At the end of the twentieth century, Internet advertising was being dismissed as a passing fad. Advertisers doubted that all those banners and pop-up pitches were accomplishing anything but annoying potential customers. Still, with almost a billion people having Internet access and about 600 million searches performed daily, there had to be *some* economic use for all this connectedness....

Then, beginning in 2000, along came some mega-billion dollar discoveries.

Google, Yahoo and other search sites realized that it was logical and lucrative to place small text-only ads adjacent to each page of search results, with the placement of ads determined by whatever search terms had been entered. For example, if you were a new parent searching for 'ecological diapers for my baby,' Google would present you with the usual pages of links to websites, just as it had done before. The change was that, on the right side of that webpage, you also saw a column of small four-line ads, similar to classified ads in a newspaper. These small ads had been paid for by advertisers who were paying for the privilege of displaying to anyone searching for 'diapers' or 'ecological + baby,' etc.

Suddenly, an advertiser could be fairly certain its ad was being shown to the right audience. Advertisers were delighted, although they wanted to pay only when someone clicked on their ad and came to the advertiser's website. Google and other search services decided to give the advertisers what they wanted, changing the basis from pay-per-view to pay-per-action. This became known as pay-per-click-through or PPC. The advertiser was paying for qualified leads only, at a few pennies each, and the idea caught on big time, soon generating billions of dollars in revenues for search engines and billions in online business for the advertisers.

Google set up an automated program that runs a continuous auction for each search word and combination of words. This program is called AdWords. Anyone – it could be an author like you – can offer 1 cent or 60 cents or $100, or whatever bid you wish, for each click-through. The advertiser offering the highest PPC gets placed at the top of the column of text ads. By adjusting the bid and watching the resulting listings, an advertiser can learn how much others are bidding for the top spots and adjust its bid accordingly. To bid and run ads, an advertiser needs to deposit money on account, in advance, with Google. Each clickthrough to the advertiser's website means the bid amount is subtracted from the money on account.

This was, and is, all quite marvelous – especially for anyone who has worked in the old direct response advertising game and who'd had to wait three months and spend $20,000 on a split run of a magazine to determine if 'New and Improved' gave a better result than 'Free $5 Coupon.' By running two simultaneous AdWords campaigns, in a kind of Internet split run, you can see the results updated every minute as real people click through to your site.

It is not too difficult to set up and manage an AdWords campaign on Google, or use the similar services called Yahoo! Search Marketing and Microsoft adCenter. Or try www.facebook.com/advertising.

Before investing much money, you will want, however, to have a way of measuring the real benefits – sales of your book, for example – and not merely how many people came to your website. Why? It may sound wonderful to be paying only 10 cents each to have people come to your book's webpage, and you therefore authorize Google to merrily eat through a $500 deposit to generate 5,000 prospects. Yet, if only 1 in 1,000 visitors to your page actually buys a book, that's only 5 books sold at an advertising cost of $500 – or $100 per book sold!

Is this a gold mine for an indie author? Probably not, unless you have a very tightly defined audience and little competition from other advertisers for those keywords. By this, I'm meaning that you might be able to pay only 1 cent per click and be attracting great prospects if you are advertising on the keywords 'building Appalachian dulcimers' (in this example, I've assumed your book has blueprints and instructions for constructing that type of dulcimer). By comparison, you might need to pay $1.50 per click for a less targeted stream of people if you were paying for the more general 'dulcimer.'

Incidentally, it is possible to select 'negative' keywords – words that you do not want. So an author advertising for that book on dulcimer-making might want 'dulcimer' but not when that word is combined with 'buy' or 'new.'

If your book is a romance novel or modern poetry, you probably cannot make keyword search advertising pay off. It will cost a fortune per click for 'romance' and you'd get millions of useless hits from love- or lust-hunting lonely souls who don't read books.

Want to buy pay-per-click or banners ads that appear on Amazon's website? Amazon sells ad space through its Clickriver subsidiary. See www.clickriver.com.

If you do have a non-fiction book, and an audience that will be using some very distinctive search words, here are two references I've used to learn more:

- *Pay-Per-Click Search Engine Marketing Handbook: Low Cost Strategies to Attracting NEW Customers Using Google, Yahoo & Other Search Engines* by Boris Mordkovich and Eugene Mordkovich [ISBN 9781411628175]

- *Pay Per Click Search Engine Marketing For Dummies* by Peter Kent [ISBN 9780471754947]

To which website will you send all those PPC customers you just paid for? You could send them to your book's page on Amazon or another online retailer. If you do, be sure to set yourself up as an Amazon Affiliate so you earn a referral fee on each sale that happens. You could send them to your book's page on the website of whichever publisher or POD service you are using. Or, you could build a dedicated website for your book – read about that in the chapter on **publicity**.

EZINE (ONLINE NEWSLETTER) AND BLOG ADVERTISING

One of the web's best kept secrets is the effectiveness of advertising in an ezine (pronounced as Eee-zeen, sometimes spelled as e-zine) or electronic magazine or newsletter. Many organizations regularly email out a digital newsletter to their members and website visitors. Because people have asked to receive information on this topic, these ezines are generally very well read and therefore provide an excellent vehicle to advertise your book to a targeted and enthused audience.

It is common for the newsletter to run an article or book review when you sign on to advertise or sponsor – be sure to ask if they will do this. The writer of the ezine has to fill space, and may be very appreciative of the expert opinions, news and credibility that you can bring. Perhaps you might offer a brief excerpt from your book that could be included as a feature or column in the newsletter.

Typically, the response (people buying your book) to an ezine ad will grow over the first few issues as people gain confidence simply by seeing it advertised repeatedly. Then, unless the readership is very large or there are new subscribers, responses may taper off. If you are tracking the response to this particular ezine, you'll know when the ad is no longer profitable. You can then suspend the paid ad for six months to a year, then try again for a few issues.

A wonderful bonus from appearing in an article and ad in an ezine/

newsletter is the boost in your personal credibility – you may be invited to speak at a conference or to consult, or be given some other opportunity in your field of expertise. Indeed, those other benefits may make up for any doubts you have about investing in specialty newsletter ads.

Blogs (short for web log) have become increasingly popular over the past few years. These are websites where someone will post frequent commentaries, similar to what a newspaper columnist might file. Some sites are now attracting regular followings of ten thousand or more readers. To advertise, contact the blog's owner. If a blog is well matched to your book's topic, paying $50 or $100 per month for exposure to all those targeted readers could prove itself worthwhile.

CHAPTER 10

Promotional mix –
publicity & public relations

*To whom will you be communicating through publicity and
how? What are the key messages?*

What publicity ideas will you implement?

Publicity is any method of informing your audience that is not
happening one-on-one (that's personal sales), and is not paid advertising. Although you aren't paying a fee directly for editorial space
or broadcast time, don't be lulled into thinking that publicity is 'free'
though – unless you consider there is no cost or value in your own labor
and that of any professional helpers you hire.

You might be amused to learn that no two Marketing professors can
agree on where *publicity* stops and *public relations* [PR] starts, although
many define PR as everything that is done to enhance the public's impression of your firm and your products. I prefer to use the rough distinc-
tion that publicity is *what you cause to happen in the media*, while PR is
more about *how you behave and what you might sponsor or endorse*. But
to keep things simple, let's call everything *publicity* in this chapter.

With publicity, you can't control what is said as you can with an advertisement. Lack of control over content, timing and even if any mention happens at all is a drawback with publicity, although that's usually outweighed by the higher credibility that a review or story has, compared to an ad. Most prospective buyers feel that a book review or feature article is unbiased, and is therefore trustworthy – which can work for or against you, depending on how the writer feels about your book!

The large publishing houses – think Random House or Simon & Schuster or Knopf – may spend hundreds of thousands of dollars for publicity each year, although only for launching expected bestsellers. For most books, their publicity budget is likely under $1,000 because publicity is notoriously hard to manage. Because high-end publicists charge a bundle to orchestrate a signing and speaking tour, media interviews and key reviews, there must be potential for selling a few hundred thousand copies before a publisher will take a really deep plunge.

The very best publicists act more like booking agents than someone begging for attention. The top ones – and most expensive and most exclusive – are so tight with producers and editors that they can simply call a producer and say, "I have a great guest for your show next Wednesday." The producer's reply would be, "Great, we'll reserve a spot. Who is it?"

Unfortunately, even if you could afford their sky-high fees, the top people won't work with unknown indie authors. You have to be a celebrity actor, politician or otherwise newsworthy character, under contract with a New York publisher. A publicist risks losing favor with his or her producer contacts if the interviewee is a dud.

Assuming you are not a 'name,' you could consider hiring a next-tier publicist or agency. Expect, however, to invest many thousands of dollars, far more than you'll likely recoup through book sale royalties. If that concept is okay for you – perhaps because you have other purposes being served by the exposure – then you might start your research by asking local journalists and TV producers to recommend a publicist they respect. Then contact that publicist, asking to create a program to match your budget and goal, whether it be local and regional exposure or getting on *Oprah!*

For about $99 per month, you can hire Dan Janal at www.PRleads. com. If you do sign up and mention my name, Dan will send you a free copy of *Guerilla Publicity* by Jay Conrad Levinson. Authors with deeper pockets could try Rick Frishman at Planned Television Arts (plannedTVarts.com). PTA will charge you a hefty $15,000 to appear on morning radio shows in key US cities – essentially you are paying for ad time although it sounds to listeners as if the DJ is interviewing you.

Another route is to buy the publicity package offered by your POD publishing service. At iUniverse, for example, authors can pay $1,500 each month, theoretically corresponding to 40 hours of a publicist's time. Purchasing a minimum of three months of service is recommended by iUniverse, plus the author pays for 30 to 100 review copies sent to the media. The author pays for mailings, while iUniverse covers phone and fax expenses. iUniverse has a clipping service that scans all print media for copies of reviews and articles about your book. Another way for authors to track media coverage is by using www.google.com/alerts.

No one can guarantee media coverage. Ultimately, whether or not the media folks are interested in the book depends solely on whether they believe at least one of the book, the topic, or the author is newsworthy.

For Jonathan Peizer, publishing *The Dynamics of Technology for Social Change: Understanding the Factors That Influence Results: Lessons Learned from the Field* [ISBN 9780595372744] was clearly about generating **publicity** and sharing best practices. His **purpose** was to establish credibility as an author and expert, and create a 'business card' for the new consultancy he was starting.

Jonathan has a very impressive background as chief information officer for George Soros's Open Society Institute. His mission there was to make information and communications technology (ICT) work for social benefit. Beginning in the early 1990s, Jonathan had a lead role in enabling Internet access across former Communist states in eastern Europe. While Soros's philanthropy was ensuring schools got computers, he was passionate about boosting – not undermining – local non-profit organizations. Soros wanted to foster grassroots innovation by not imposing preconceived 'outside' solutions. For exam-

ple, Jonathan's book describes how the city of Riga in Latvia was using a city-wide wireless area network in the early 1990s, more than a decade before this was being rolled out in the West.

Academics and executives at non-profits and foundations who need to better understand the motivations and dynamics around implementing ICT for social change are the **public** for Jonathan's book. *Knowledge* about what works in real life and what doesn't, in order to avoid costly failures, is really the **product** being sold. There are no other books on this subject written by a practitioner with Jonathan's level of experience, and especially someone known for successes with the Soros Foundation (the unique sales proposition or **positioning**).

Jonathan arranged distribution (**place**) through his publisher: availability at all the major online retailers in paperback and eBook editions. His promotional mix focused on **publicity**. One hundred copies were sent to practitioners in the field to create word-of-mouth recommendations. Three experts posted 5-star reviews on Amazon.com. A staff publicist hired through iUniverse worked at generating media interest, while news release services added to the buzz. A mailing was sent out to universities, aimed at faculty and researchers in this field.

Jonathan took advantage of being well networked; he sent out an announcement to 2,000 people in his personal and professional contact list. He also wrote a blog and promoted the book on lists and at websites, such as technologyforsocialchange.com, internautconsulting.com and capaciteria.com (he is a founder and director of the last organization).

Has Jonathan made a fortune on royalties? "Not enough to make an overall **profit**. I spent $8,000 in all on promotion, books to give away, editing, etc., but it was a business write-off and has had other benefits outside of straight sales. It provides credibility. A year later people are still buying copies as well. I understood from the start I was writing for a rather specialized audience; it's not Harry Potter."

An Internet search on his name provides over 20,000 results, so the publicity goal has been attained – and his consultancy is doing well.

This book is designed to help society (**people**) and the **planet**. It was written to "help people harness and use their resources more effectively and efficiently," says Jonathan. "Through technology, environmental, educational, health and political information can be shared more easily for positive social change."

Even if publicity isn't going to be one of the Ps emphasized in your marketing mix, there are two basic publicity tasks that are so effective that you'd be foolish to skip them. These activities can be summed up as follows:

1. start locally with community newspapers and broadcast media to get your very first reviews or features. Then send those results to regional, then national reviewers and journalists.
2. get reviews posted at Amazon.com.

A clear demonstration of the benefit of the above two-part, minimalist publicity program was the great start and continuing sales longevity for Bradley Fenton's book, *Stumbling Naked in the Dark: Overcoming Mistakes Men Make With Women* [ISBN 9781412012157]. Brad lives in Florida and first focused on the local Palm Beach newspaper.

"I called first and they said send it in. I asked for the name of the person who would read it so I could leave them a message. That's important so he or she knows there is a real human being behind it. Local journalists have an emotional attachment to people in their community, and an obligation to report local stuff to make up the news. Reporters are just ordinary people whose job is to fill space.

"I wrote my book from the heart – you have to have faith in your book. It was timely. After I got two large newspaper articles, I sent out a press release and media kit with the *Palm Beach Post* article to everyone I knew and to regional media."

Brad takes copies of *Stumbling Naked in the Dark* to sell at his speaking engagements, even when the topic is sales training or other motivational concepts. People do buy copies in person, though his main outlet has been Amazon.com.

"I sent copies to friends, and urged them to write honest reviews on Amazon.com. That's very important, that the review is honest. A good review can really help; it makes sales and also creates links to and from other books on the same or related topics. With enough links to other books, your book sells forever," Brad says.

"My book got a link on the page for *The Game* and other bestsellers, suggesting customers buy both books together, so that was incredible publicity for me when *The Game* was so big."

Having Amazon customers see Brad's book recommended when they search for better-known titles was enough to sell 6,000 copies in three years, notes Brad, with almost no other promotions or publicity happening!

Amazon actually has a mechanism where you can pay to have your book shown as a recommended purchase on another book's page. It is their 'Buy X, Get Y (BXGY Paid Placement) Program'. *[This would fall under paid advertising or sales promotions in our 14-P mix.]* Go to www.amazon.com/publishers to get pricing. A caution about the effectiveness of BXGY is registered by Aaron Shepard in his indie book, *Aiming at Amazon* [ISBN 9780938497431]. Aaron says, "In almost every case, BXGY will cost you more money than you make from it."

It is widely reported that acquisition editors at publishing houses will give larger advances on a publishing contract if you can demonstrate that you can generate publicity. They will do Internet searches and also look at your newspaper tear sheets. So how can you boost your rankings on Internet searches? By having your name *everywhere*.

Dan Janal at PRleads.com warns that once you stop doing publicity and other promotions, it is like turning off the tap for sales. He urges authors to build a networking emailing list. When you get some coverage, send a cheery announcement to everyone.

Eric Gruber is so keen on spreading your message and building your 'expert' status, that he's developed a service for placing short articles you write all over the web – for a fee, of course. He'll find websites hungry for articles that match your specialty, whether it is model trains, poetry, parenting, military history or local hiking trails. Check out his service at articlemarketingexperts.com. Each month you give Eric one article and $500, and his staff will look after finding all the related ezines, blog spots and article sites (such as About.com) and submitting your how-to tips, FAQs or whatever.

You can do these submissions yourself if your budget is tight, though it takes lots of time to figure out the processes. Start by using a search engine to find which are the top information websites your target audience would be directed to. When you submit articles, you won't get paid, but you'll gain links to your own website and to buying your book at online retailers. Beside each article will be an author blurb where your credibility as an expert is touted (you write this).

You can also build exposure and notoriety by responding to others' writings on blogs.

Dan figures that 80% of all journalists are now finding experts online to quote or interview for stories. If you don't have many expert citations on the net, you won't be found and quoted in other media.

Eric suggests you re-cycle the articles into a free newsletter to send to your ever-growing email networking list.

DIY PUBLICITY IN LOCAL, THEN REGIONAL, THEN NATIONAL MEDIA

Many years ago I worked as a reporter at a community newspaper. Occasionally I'd get volunteered by the editor to review a book by a local author. Even though that experience was back in the days of using typewriters, the personal dynamics haven't changed and I can vouch for the following tips as still being valid for today's indie author:

- it is more valuable and often easier to be featured in a column or lifestyle section article – rather than having your book reviewed – as long as there is some interesting angle to your situation. Think about 'soccer mom's poetry book dream comes true' or 'local blacksmith shares old-time tips using new-fangled publishing.'

- collect names of local journalists who cover stories similar to yours. With all the frantic activity at a newspaper or TV station, generic 'Dear Editor' submissions may go directly into the trash. Before you mail anything, call the receptionist and confirm the name, phone number and mailing address.

- use your network of friends, business colleagues and neighbors. See who has connections to the media. Most journalists respond well to tips from people they know, since there is a requirement to fill a lot of space and air time every day!

- when sending in your book, include a press release and author bio. Be sure to ask for what you want – an article or a review – since it may not be obvious to the person opening the package.

- follow-up with a phone call in a few days to check that the book arrived and got to the right person. This is a prime moment to offer to be interviewed on the phone, so the journalist gets a fresh quote for the article, or a radio person gets their 'sound bite.'

- if it seems that a receptionist is acting as a gatekeeper, then shamelessly suck up. Remember her name. Send her chocolates as a bribe (thanking her and her colleagues for doing such a great job of reporting to the community). Keep your cool – she's just doing her job.

- keep a list and keep calling. Because books or story tips that are deep in the pile will never get used, your purpose is to make sure your book gets put back on the top of that pile every time you call.

- if a local bookstore has agreed to carry copies of your book, ask the manager for his/her publicity contacts at local media outlets. It helps to be able to say to a journalist that the local Barnes & Noble manager wants the store mentioned in the article – this is an implied endorsement by someone in the book trade.

- once you've had an article or review published in one paper, take that to the local competition and to regional media. Then take regional story clippings to national media.

If you have an outgoing personality, you might do well simply by arriving at a newspaper and declaring that you are there to be interviewed by Mr. So-and-so (insert name of the Editor) or someone he assigns. As we described in a previous chapter, Georgina Cronin [*Size Matters – Especially When You Weigh 330 lbs*; ISBN 1553955595] had wonderful publicity success by showing up unscheduled at newspaper offices. Georgina, who had worked in advertising and other media jobs, has a commanding presence and carried off this 'of course you'll interview me' approach masterfully. She knew a full-length 'now' picture and the unflattering 'before' shot were perfect for full-page feature articles in the popular papers.

An author with the knack for impromptu speaking may wish to contact local talk radio stations, offering himself or herself as a last-minute guest available to fill in on short notice. When a scheduled guest can't be connected, you'll be a lifesaver for the host. Keep a sheet handy with all the important points you want to get in during your interview. Be sure to mention your book's title and where to buy it! If you have a website, ask the host to include it in the intro and 'outro.'

Two decades later and now living a quite, respectable suburban life with a husband and two sons, Elizabeth Hudson felt compelled to tell the story of her early life as a heroin addict who turned to prostitution for survival. Her **purpose** was two-fold: to educate and warn readers, and to establish herself as a professional writer. Encouraged and mentored by bestselling crime-writer Marion Rippon, Elizabeth found writing to be both cathartic and terrifying. When she could not interest a mainstream publishing house in the manuscript, she paid to self-publish through a print-on-demand service.

But how would she get anyone's attention? Elizabeth decided to use **publicity** wherever possible. She hounded the media for reviews and, at one point, stood at the side of a busy Calgary thoroughfare at rush hour with a large sign urging commuters to BUY MY BOOK!

Within months, the power of her writing and her persistent presence in the media caught the attention of NeWest Press, who signed Elizabeth to a publishing contract. NeWest insisted on an extensive re-write, changing a narrated novel into a riveting, utterly honest first-person account. They also set up an extensive **publicity** tour, with Elizabeth traveling to many cities and sometimes speaking at fund-raisers for organizations helping sex-trade workers.

Her book, *Snow Bodies: One Woman's Life on the Street* [NeWest Press, ISBN 9781896300740], was nominated for many literary awards. Elizabeth has since published articles and poetry in national magazines.

Back in 1987, my wife and I helped a minister from Wingham, Ontario, independently publish *Moods and Thoughts for Today* [ISBN 0969320906]. Over the previous few years, Rev. Douglas Whitelaw had prepared and honed 150 daily meditations on Bible scriptures. Each one had been delivered from the pulpit and also broadcast on radio CKNX FM-102 on Douglas's weekly show called *Moods and Thoughts for a Sunday.*

Of course, Douglas had a natural marketing tactic: **publicity**. He could mention the book each week in the intro and outro of his broadcast. He could also mention it at his church. With congregation members spreading the news about his book, Douglas sold lots of books and spread the word (the Holy word, that is) – which was his **purpose**. Four years ago, when my mother died, I found a copy of Douglas's book on her nightstand, with her penciled comments in the margins. Apparently her Bible study group had discussed some of the meditations. It is lovely how books have such wide and lasting impact.

FREE PRESS RELEASE DISTRIBUTION

You can expect little-to-no immediate response from the media to a press release sent out as a general email broadcast to all media everywhere. And you can also count on getting your contact information onto every spammer's list to sell you Viagra and sure-fire Nigerian investment opportunities! However, if you are banking on the concept of getting as much exposure as possible for free, you could devote a few days to sending out releases through the many free or almost-free distribution services. These sites send out so many releases per day that I expect all media now block any email originating from them, but the releases do get indexed by search engines, adding a few more links to your website. Who knows? A journalist might someday find your contact info in a last-minute hunt for an expert to quote, and you'll get a few minutes of unexpected fame. Here are a few sites:

Free-Press-Release.com	PR.com
PRFree.com	PRLeap.com

PRWeb.com   i-NewsWire.com

SBWire.com   TheOpenPress.com

WebWire.com

Since most media outlets are flooded with releases every day, you'd be wise to hand-deliver yours if at all possible. Or do anything else to set yours apart, even if it seems over the top. If you've written a cookbook, send it in with cookies! If it is a novel about horse-racing, how about enclosing tickets to the race-track, or a wager slip? Could you invite the reporter to an event – perhaps the book launch? Anything to break the dull monotony of press releases that read 'local man writes book' and 'new poetry book published.'

What should a press release look like? There are two basic types – let's call them the traditional and the flyer – and experts disagree about which works best at generating interviews and articles. By the way, the terms *press release, news release* and *media release* are all used inter-changeably by journalists.

The traditional press release format is shown on the opposite page (adapted from PRWeb.com). See an example of a flyer-style release at: *www.agiopublishing.com/authors/valpattee/VPatteePressRelease.pdf.*

A press release written in flyer format serves as a brochure or pro-motion of the author's availability as an interview subject. You have the same info as in the traditional release, but add in a splashy color photo of the author and a list of typical interview topics. Ten Top Tips for Publish-ing Your Poetry; How I Overcame Writer's Block and You Can Too; 100 Ways to Leave Your Lover; Nine Ways to Bake Dynamite Apple Cobbler that will save your marriage, whatever. The hope is that a producer or DJ will be so enthralled that you'll get a few minutes of air time to talk enthusiastically about the ten tips or nine ways, and can slip in a mention of your book. Remember that the focus of the flyer release is not your book – it's your entertainment value in an interview where you'll men-tion your book. When crafting a press release, the key question is 'who

Headline Announces News in Title Case, Ideally Under 80 Characters

A summary or synopsis paragraph, elaborating on the news in the headline in one or two sentences. This summary uses sentence case, with standard capitalization and punctuation.

For Immediate Release

City, State – Month 1, 2007 – The lead sentence contains the most important information in 25 words or less. Grab your reader's attention here by simply stating the news you have to announce. Do not assume that your reader has read your headline or summary paragraph; the lead should stand on its own. The first paragraphs should answer the who, what, when, where, why and how questions – and the all-important 'why bother to read this.'

A press release, like a newspaper story, keeps sentences and paragraphs short, about three or four lines per paragraph. Journalists may take information from a press release to craft a news or feature article, and may use some of it word-for-word.

The rest of the release expounds on the information provided in the lead paragraph. It includes quotes from the author or subject matter experts. It contains more details about the news you have to tell, which can be about something unique or controversial or about a prominent person, place or thing.

The tone is neutral and objective, not full of hype or text that is typically found in an advertisement. Avoid directly addressing the consumer or your target audience. The use of the first person or second person ('I', 'you' or 'we') outside of a direct quotation is a flag that this is an advertisement rather than a press release.

The standard press release is 300 to 800 words. Always check the spelling and grammar before submission.

For additional information (or for a sample, copy or demo), contact author Mary Smith or visit www.xxxxx.com. You can also include details on product availability, trademark acknowledgment, etc., here.

About Author Mary Smith

Include a short backgrounder or 'boilerplate' about the author, stressing the newsworthy aspects.

Contact

Mary Smith, author
Address, city, state, phone number, website

cares?' You must figure out if anyone would care about you and your 'news.' Then decide why it matters to them. Once you've answered those questions, you can start writing the headlines and body copy with those people in mind.

Many indie authors lament that reviewers in major newspapers and magazines tend to pass over new indie books in favor of releases from the big publishing houses. Sometimes it takes one good review to prime the pump; by including one published review with your submission, you are assuring the reviewer that he or she is not going totally out on a limb by being the very first to comment on your book. To get that first review, you can send a finished copy (not a proof or a galley) of your book plus the press release to James A. Cox, Midwest Book Review, 278 Orchard Drive, Oregon, WI, USA 535751129. Their website is www.midwest-bookreview.com. Jim Cox's volunteer reviewers give preference to independently published books. We appreciate that, Jim!

Your own webpage & website

Most publishing services will provide a webpage with information about an author's books and include a mechanism for customers to purchase these books – either directly on that site or through links to major online booksellers. Having a webpage with e-commerce capability is essential so you can have sales happening 24 hours a day.

Some authors create whole websites devoted to their book, where they will provide in-depth information about their book's topic. The more information there is on the site, the more likely it will be referenced prominently on major search sites such as Yahoo! and Google. You can add an online bookstore quite simply by becoming an Amazon Affiliate (Amazon Associate in Canada and UK) and hosting an Amazon aStore on your own website. After you insert the few lines of HTML code, presto, your website is a 24/7 e-commerce enterprise with you earning an extra 4% commission on top of your regular royalties for Amazon sales.

Guerrilla Marketing for Financial Advisors [ISBN 1412003997] was written by Grant Hicks and Jay Conrad Levinson, author of the highly successful *Guerrilla Marketing* series of books. Grant and Jay set up an elaborate website for their book that included articles to supplement the book, press releases, testimonials and, most importantly, links to Amazon.com and a host of other online retailers where the book could be purchased.

The website provided two free chapters and the ability to subscribe to a newsletter that Grant sent out on a regular basis. Both of these freebies required visitors to provide their email address. By capturing email addresses, Grant and Jay were able to promote other services such as Grant's seminars and Jay's other books.

Within months of the release of his book, Grant was the victim of his own success, as his life became a blur of travel for speaking engagements and media promotions, mixed with writing more fresh content for the website and newsletters. I got glimpses of this whirlwind as Grant's publisher and through my parents who used him as their personal financial advisor. After two years, he wisely took a step back in order, in his words, "to get my life back and spend time with my family" and re-focus on his booming retirement planning business. "I just got too busy, and needed to take control of life first, business second."

Because demands on Grant's time to maintain his website, online promotions and travel for presentations got so intense, "I had to cut back on the successful marketing ideas that worked too well!"

Thousands of financial planners now use Grant's marketing system. He's planning to write and promote another book, but limits his travel and speaking commitments. Grant has this advice for authors: "Plan for growth and expansion instead of reacting to it."

Clearly, maintaining an elaborate website consumes a lot of time. Grant's experience illustrates that occasionally an author's marketing mix can become *so* potent that it is wise to dampen it down, changing some of the Ps to ensure you are meeting all of your life's **purposes**.

GETTING PEOPLE TO VISIT YOUR WEBSITE

Visitors to your website will come because they've seen the web address in some printed material or at another website, or through searching at Yahoo! or Google or other sites. You can also pay for online advertising (see chapter on **paid advertising**) such as those text-only AdWords that appear on search sites and across the web.

Whether or not you pay for online ads, there are many free ways to boost the popularity of your site. Doing a search on your book's topic will show you which websites are currently popular – it is on those websites where you want links for your site. Send an email to any address that appears (even the webmaster for that site could be helpful), and ask for a book review or referral link. Each external link to your webpage will boost your site's likelihood of being shown in response to a search. Many niche website owners are thrilled to email back and forth with new enthusiasts and may provide glowing reviews and testimonials for you to use in your publicity kit.

Most webpages get indexed by search engines that have automated programs that systematically follow every link on every page they encounter, reading all the words in the HTML coding that makes up a webpage. By going from webpage to webpage, these 'knowbots' or 'spiders' reach billions of pages and come back regularly to look for changes. The knowbots are recording and indexing every word displayed on the webpage, as well as the metadata tags in the underlying HTML code header. You can submit a webpage's address (URL) to Google and other search engines if you are impatient waiting for knowbots to show up.

You can hire a search engine optimization (SEO) specialist to help optimize your website so it shows prominently for certain keywords. Note, however, that no one can deliver permanent top ranking results because of the ever-changing algorithms at the search companies. Most

SEO specialists can also run a pay-per-click advertising campaign for you, if you wish to try that form of Internet **paid advertising**.

A general resource on the topic of search engine advertising, optimization and Internet marketing in general is searchenginewatch.com.

Forums (newsgroups, message boards) and Blogs

Internet forums (also called newsgroups and message or bulletin boards) and blogs (short for web-log or weblog) are simply messages posted under a categorization or common topic.

Newsgroups/forums/boards have been around since the beginning of the Internet. Information is usually organized by topics called 'threads.' Sometimes one person will post a question to start a thread, and many different people will respond with answers or comments. Yahoo is one of many companies that host thousands of groups you can join (groups. yahoo.com).

By contrast, a blog is like an Internet diary with most entries posted by a single individual, generally with an option for readers to post their responses. Check out www.blogger.com (run by Google).

Advertising within these forms of 'social networking' is in its relative infancy, but there are opportunities to post relevant information or questions to groups while including a discrete message about your book in your *sig* or signature block at the end.

Often those who use groups are extremely dedicated to their topic of interest, and some are active and influential in similar groups. If you can get good reviews posted by group users, word spreads fast and it can go a long way to driving sales.

Hank Hagquist, co-author of *Big Jim's RC Motor Black Book* [ISBN 9781553690863], watched sales for his indie book grow as he posted answers to remote controlled car enthusiasts' questions on hobbyist newsgroups. Hank provided expert advice and information while also discretely including the name of his book and where to purchase a copy in his signature block.

Here are some basic tips about posting comments on a group or forum, or at someone's blog:

- include insightful information, not just 'buy my book'
- check the forum's policy about including in your sig actual hyperlinks to a retail site where your book is on sale, since some frown on this
- don't type in ALL CAPS as people automatically assume that you are ANGRY and RANTING
- write in short sentences with frequent paragraph breaks since the default layout of most forums is already hard to read
- be aware that these posts will be publicly available (indexed on Google, Yahoo and elsewhere) *forever*, so include your best information, don't criticize anyone unfairly and check your spelling before clicking on the submit button
- include in your comments the keywords you hope your potential target audience will be searching
- in your sig have a short statement about your book – the elevator pitch in ten words!

One trend is to use a blog to record one's writing progress and hopefully generate a following of individuals who are waiting to buy the book once it is finished. If you collect their email addresses, you will be able to announce the launch widely and possibly cause an immediate surge in buying that could be noticed within the book trade.

Though he is not an indie author, it is worth noting the example of *Wired Magazine*'s editor, Chris Anderson, who created a huge advance buzz about *The Long Tail: Why the Future of Business Is Selling Less of More* [ISBN 9781401302375]. He collected email addresses at his personal blog website called www.thelongtail.com. When the book launched in

2006, it immediately jumped to the top of the bestseller charts. Although it certainly helped that Chris was able to also promote his theories and forthcoming book in *Wired*, he does credit his blog for the rapid start to sales and publicity.

Many authors are now trying to create an advance demand through a Facebook and Twitter presence. Some pundits predict author blogs and social networking (Facebook, MySpace, etc.) will eventually replace bookstore signing tours and in-person appearances. I don't agree, but do think a blog is simple, effective publicity. WordPress.com and Blogger.com provide free services that make it easy to get started. At Agio Publishing House, we use WordPress software to host blogs for me (www.bookmarketing.agiopublishing.com) and other authors on our own websites.

Interested in more info about publicizing through blogs and other online social networking? Check out Steve Weber's informative indie book *Plug Your Book: Online Book Marketing for Authors, Book Publicity through Social Marketing* [ISBN 9780977240616].

What's the newest publicity tactic for books? Video trailers. Make a short intriguing commercial using iMovie, post it on YouTube and hope it gets lots of exposure on YouTube.com and is passed around in emails.

After a year of publicizing his history book, *Turkey's Modernization: Refugees from Nazism and Atatürk's Vision* [ISBN 0977790886], Prof. Arnold Reisman has come to view the publicity process as similar to scientific models for the spread of highly infectious disease or ripples in a pond. When your book is mentioned at one website or in an academic journal, that occurrence will be cited in search engines, blogs and what he calls 'parasite sites' (websites that automatically troll the web for new content to reproduce in hopes of attracting readers and generating

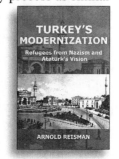

advertising revenue). Each mention sets off a small ripple that becomes a wave that, combined with all the other waves, can result in a tidal wave of awareness. Arnold says his book "is reviewed – or at least mentioned – on a multitude of websites the differentiated URLs of which fill 110 single-spaced 8.5" by 11" pages. They represent at least 31 countries, and appear in at least nine different languages."

What caused some of the more productive ripples? Arnold contributed new history articles at the sometimes maligned but widely used Wikipedia.org, and added information to existing articles, always citing his book as a reference. These posting were picked up by numerous databases, such as Google, Yahoo, blogs and all those parasites. Far larger waves were generated by three articles Arnold wrote for the *History News Network* – newspapers in several countries picked these up. Arnold can trace waves (requests for review copies) from simply having his book's reference and cover image in his own email signature. One such review was in *Nature*, the prestigious and widely-quoted British magazine. From that exposure he was invited to contribute chapters to new books and to present at a conference in Poland. Now, by being mentioned in *Book Marketing DeMystified: Self-Publishing Success*, Arnold's book will be cross-referenced by Amazon.com and others. Clearly the spread of awareness – and opportunity – does appear infectious, in a very good way!

I hope the stories of other authors and the explanations have got you thinking about how to **publicize** your book. Some of the ideas discussed require someone who is very comfortable with public speaking. If that is not you, there are other tactics that will be more suited to you and your situation. The key is to decide which Ps to emphasize, which ones to pass on – and mostly to have fun.

CHAPTER 11

Promotional mix – sales promotions

*What will you do as a **sales promotion** for your book?*

*What are your ideas for **push promotions** that will encourage distributors and retailers to stock and sell your book?*

*How will you bring customers to the retail outlets? (**pull promotions**)*

*Can your book be used as a **sales promotion** for other products or services?*

Marketing people tend to divide **sales promotions** into two categories: **push** promotions and **pull** promotions. Think of a hypothetical widget company that manufactures a product (the hypothetical widget!) and sends it down a distribution 'pipeline' to retail stores where customers make a purchase. Any way to stuff more product down that pipeline or ease the friction would be a *push tactic*. Any means of creating a demand for the product at the far end is like creating a vacuum that *pulls* the stream of widget products through that pipe.

Push promotions make it more worthwhile and/or easier for distributors and retailers to get lots of your product into the retail outlets and on display. For example, giving the distributor and/or retailer a higher margin or buying shelf space would give your book priority over competing titles. Offering free shipping could be an incentive to the retailer to order in and feature your book. Holding a contest granting the top selling store a trip to Hawaii might be a bit over your budget, but you get the idea. Simply showing up to do an exciting signing event or in-store seminar might be a push strategy, if the manager believes that this will be lucrative for the store.

Bestselling authors Joan Bidinosti and Marilyn Wearring [*Muffins: A Cookbook*; ISBN 0969134509], whom we profiled earlier, found that stores sold more copies if provided with an attractive cardboard display. They cleverly designed the fold-up display so it would serve double-duty as a packing case. When a vendor ordered at least 20 copies, they received the stand for free. That's an example of a **push** tactic.

Any display or signage in a store is referred to as POP or point-of-purchase materials. Perhaps you could provide bookmarks?

It is 100% okay to simply ask your distributor or some store managers what would motivate them best. If you and they together can find solutions, it will be a win-win situation. In the discussions, clearly state that your goal is to launch a multi-year success for everyone.

Pull promotions make people come to a store to buy your product. Coupons and samples are common examples. Brand awareness advertising and publicity also function as pull sales promotions. Whatever you do to encourage customers to come to the store and buy is *pull*.

Remember Fred and Peg Francis who wrote *Democratic Rules of Order: The Complete Official Parliamentary Authority for Meetings of Any Size* [ISBN 096992604] with the noble **purpose** of having *everyone* at meetings understand the rules, not just a few? They needed to have a few influential people working as evangelists for their book, so they sent out 2,000 sample copies, targeting municipal government clerks, church leaders, librarians and others. Providing free **samples** was a **pull sales promotion** that created a demand for the book, causing orders to flow in to Fred Francis's home and to retailers.

Sometimes a book can itself be the promotion or sample for some other product or service. Broadcast Hall of Fame member Lynn Tolliver Jr. has written many controversial short books [see *The Best of Lynn Tolliver, Jr.*; ISBN 1552122182]. While he was a big-time radio personality in Cleveland, Lynn would give away copies of his books as a prize to listeners.

The books were samples of his often-outrageous views on topics such as prenuptial contracts, President Clinton's sex controversy and Ebonics (*Idionics* according to Tolliver). Having these books in circulation helped **promote** his radio show by building his brand (**positioning**) and vice versa.

Cartoonist Joe King's indie books are part of his overall **positioning** (branding) as an illustrator, cartoonist, book designer and marketing producer. His syndicated cartoon strip is published in California newspapers, his caricatures are treasured artwork, and his lifestyle is cartoon-character chaotic. Joe publishes collections of cartoons in books – then re-purposes the artwork onto mugs and shirts sold through CafePress.com. Joe can pass out a coffee mug or a book when **promoting** his syndicated  strip. His signature on the cartoons takes readers to his website to buy books or mugs that **promote** his strips, and round and round. One of Joe's books is *Funny Paperz #4: Bestest Editorial Cartoons of the Year – 2005* [ISBN 1412099196]. Check out how he merges and morphs the marketing mix at his website www.funnypaperz.com.

Another spot where you can have your book's cover or other art produced on t-shirts, mugs, posters, etc. is Zazzle.com.

Do you feel your novel ought to appeal to book club members, and only needs some word-of-mouth buzz to get started? How about considering **sampling** – a form of sales promotion? You know that a shampoo manufacturer wouldn't launch a product without sending small samples to every home, right? Most libraries now stock some books in reading group sets of 7 copies. You could donate a few sample sets, and include in the back of each copy a note asking for comments to be sent to you via email. If a group loves your book, the news will quickly fan out to their network of relatives and friends.

Los Angeles-based writer Mark Jeffrey has created a six-book series, starting with *Max Quick Book One: The Pocket and the Pendant*, [ISBN 9781411613232] which he self-published through Lulu.com. Mark's

product is a combination of fantasy and sci-fi carefully crafted to, in his words:

a)   appeal to both adults and young adults, as did *Star Wars* and *Harry Potter*

b)   explore the metaphysical underpinnings of the universe ("The rules of my fictional world are that the external world is somehow an expression of all of our internal worlds collectively.")

c)   present a puzzle world with a "rich mythology like *X-Files* or *Lost*, where there are plans within plans, surprise parentages and relationships," and

d)   even if you didn't get any of the above, still be "a kick-ass story with lots of cool action, funny snappy dialogue, plot twists and neat artifacts."

Obviously Mark is not alone in wanting to break into this market. Thousands of writers aspire to have a famous series that becomes a string of movies. How would he break out of the pack?

He tried various types of paid advertising, such as Google AdWords and banner ads on websites, determining the only success was with Amazon's Better Together program. "When Amazon suggests you buy book X with book Y, that is a paid-for pairing although they do not make this obvious," says Mark. "You select a book thematically similar to your own and apply to be paired with it for a month. Bestsellers are $750/month, lesser sellers are $500. You might be accepted, you might not. Books like *Harry Potter*, *The Da Vinci Code*, etc. are booked months – sometimes years – in advance. Also, you might be rejected if your book X is nothing like book Y so far as Amazon can tell. But, if you get in, this works very, very well."

Yet Mark's real marketing breakthrough wasn't something he paid for – it was free **publicity** that could also be classified as providing **free samples**, a form of **pull sales promotion**.

"I created a blog and website at www.pocketandpendant.com. I answered inbound emails," says Mark. "But the biggest thing I did by far was to create a podcast audiobook or 'podiobook' version of my book -- and give it away for free. Evo Terra, who runs www.podiobooks.com, convinced me to do this in early 2005. It was a massive success, getting over 1.5 million downloads within two years. Many purchasers of the paperback said they bought the print version for someone because they loved the podiobook. *Max Quick Book One* remains a freely available podiobook at www.podiobooks.com.

What does success [**purpose**] look like for Mark in both intangible and tangible forms? I asked and here is his emailed reply:

"Did I feel like I accomplished what I meant to? Is the story something I would want to read? Is it different enough from other things out there (by this I mean original)? So far, I feel that I have accomplished that.

"Secondarily, is it popular? Do people like it? The printed book version of *The Pocket and the Pendant* has been moderately successful (sales of over 3,500 copies in the first two years), but it's the podcast audiobook version that's been the huge success. I haven't made a lot of money off either, but I have built a large audience and brand. Future Max

Quick undertakings – the next books, movies, big publishing deal – will hopefully be more financially successful. :) "

Mark spent only $2,000 in total to get that far, and has recouped all his financial investment. While he writes the other Max Quick books, Mark receives a modest stream of royalties from the paperback sales and up to $80 per month in spontaneous donations from listeners to the podiobook episodes. [**profit planning**]

He gives credit to many others who have helped him [**partners**]: "Podiobooks.com and Evo Terra, of course. Evo really was the main cheerleader, using his DragonPage show to promote myself, Scott Sigler, Tee Morris, Mur Lafferty and Matthew Wayne Selznick. In addition, I got myself interviewed by other podcasters, such as Soccergirl and Incorporated. They're always looking for guests, so it wasn't too hard. Lulu.com has itself been very helpful."

Mark doesn't know the exact correlation, but suspects that about half of his overall print sales are because of the podcasts. As each new book in the series is launched, Mark Jeffrey's **publicity** and **free sampling sales promotion** machine will only grow stronger.

Although this isn't an example from the self-publishing side, the following anecdote does illustrate a brilliant use of sampling to promote books. Back in 1989, while most of us were watching on our TV sets as the Berlin Wall came down, sales reps from the publisher of *Harlequin Romance* books were rushing tens of thousands of copies from their warehouses to the breaches in the border. As East German women returned to their homes after a glorious visit to West Berlin, the sales reps handed out free romance novels. The novels had been not allowed by the old East German regime, and quickly became widely popular in that newly-liberated market. The samples gave Harlequin a significant jump on their competition.

CHAPTER 12

Profits

What are your financial goals and constraints?

Have you prepared a budget?

*Is your commitment of money and time sustainable,
knowing that a mix will succeed only if you can
consistently apply the required resources? (Perhaps the
fifteenth P could be 'Persistence'!)*

W here marketing gets tricky for the novice author is deciding what you can do and, more importantly, which activities *not* to do. If you surf the web, you can very quickly be drawn in by some flashy businesses – they are using quite sophisticated, digital hype and hard-sell – who want to entice you into spending a fortune on their particular marketing solution. You *must* build a frenetic website like theirs; you *should* become a relentlessly self-promoting expert who travels the country giving motivational presentations at conventions; you *will* buy dozens of how-to books and reports to learn more from self-styled experts; you *have* to buy the deluxe/platinum/monster promotional package that will cost tens of thousands of dollars and boost your ego (and little else).

You *need* to buy this DVD for only $399.00 – special price today only, of course – or sign up for a seminar and coaching (or attend a publishing university!) for a mere $6,000 or $10,000. Exclusive, but you qualify today only! Whew!

What defense does a newcomer have to all this polished persuasion: this carefully calculated brew of guilt and temptation? It is seductive to be told that it is your destiny to conquer the literary world, and the only hurdle is investing a huge amount so you can then become the famously wealthy author of the next *Chicken Soup for the Soul* or *Harry Potter*. And certainly there are 101, or 1001, ways to promote your book – you will feel pressure and guilt if you don't do them all....

The best defense is to sit down *long before* you start your marketing campaign and commit to the most important decision:

How much time and money do I want to invest towards achieving my purpose?

Most writers have a day job. All of us have certain financial obligations: paying rent or a mortgage, saving for retirement and holidays, putting food on the table, etc. Everyone has a family or at least a social network that needs attention. People have individual commitments to the community that usually bring some well-earned satisfaction. Likely you've already 'borrowed' heavily from the rest of your life, both in time and in money, to write your book over the last few months or years.

It will take a bit of soul-searching. Yet it is important to write down some specifics – an actual number of hours per month and an amount of cash per year – to invest in marketing your book. To be safe, assume that you will receive *nothing* in royalties and sales margins, so that you can plan for the worst-case scenario and anything better is 'gravy.'

I suggest that you write those time and money limits on a big sign, to post near your desk. Then make up a list of the other assets you can apply to the marketing task – assets such as the email addresses of 50 friends, contacts in the local media, a relative who works in a bookstore, membership in a church or service club, etc.

Then you can go over the list of Ps to see what are the most appropriate marketing strategies and how you will pay for them in hours, dollars and other assets.

- Purpose/passion
- Place (distribution & timing)
- Price/value
- Partnerships
- Paid Advertising
- Sales Promotions
- Planet

- Product or Service
- Public(s)
- Positioning
- Personal Sales
- Publicity & Public Relations
- Profits
- People

Are you wondering what is the norm to spend on marketing by the 'professionals' in the mainstream publishing houses? It seems that book publishers are very tight, compared to those in other creative fields. Spending $20,000 to promote an individual title is a significant commitment. Spending over $100,000 is uncommon. Very, very few books would have a seven-figure marketing budget.

Compare this to the Hollywood film industry where it is common to spend as much on advertising and other promotions as is budgeted for the production of the entire movie itself. A $35 million film can have another $35 million spent on promotions. (Even India's Bollywood films have marketing commitments at 15% to 40% of the total budget.) The huge gap between promotional spending on movies and on books helps explain why movie companies have bought up book publishers, rather than vice versa. The media conglomerates do their book promotions as a sideline to, or market test for, the 'reel event' (the movie).

When you are writing your manuscript, getting it published and marketing it, keep track of every expense slip. They add up quickly, and are tax deductible in most jurisdictions since you are working on a business enterprise that has a reasonable expectation of profit, right? Of course, you'd better check with an accountant before submitting too large a claim on your taxes.

Although your accountant may cringe at this advice, I'll give it anyway: as you set out on this new enterprise of being a self-publishing (and self-marketing) author, set up your bookkeeping on a 'cash basis.' This is simpler and more intuitive than an accrual method. You record a sale only when you get paid, and record an expense when you incur it. Pay every expense right away. If you do otherwise and accrue your expenses (liabilities) to pay later, you might get lulled into thinking that everything in that bank account is yours to keep! Recording your sales orders before you actually get paid is like counting your chickens before they hatch.

How many books do typical self-publishing authors sell? It is amazingly difficult to get specifics from any of the publishing services. The large retailers can't provide figures by type of publisher since no one keeps or is willing to share those statistics. I've been pioneering in the print-on-demand field since its inception, and believe the following to be fairly accurate....

An author paying a publishing service that charges almost no set-up fee (and generally provides little hand-holding and few services), such as Lulu.com, CafePress.com or Blurb.com, will likely buy less than 5 copies himself/herself on average over the lifespan of the book, and sell only one or 2 copies through retailers.

Authors paying considerably more for a more personalized service with more benefits, such as light editing, typesetting, cover design, ISBN and distribution through Ingram's network (examples would be Author-House, Xlibris, SpirePublishing.com, Trafford, etc.) will buy on average 125 books, including the copies included in any package deal, and on average, sell about 45 copies through retail channels.

Using the above statistics, you can estimate conservative, 'reasonable case' royalties and margins on sales. You can find the cost of publishing at the individual services' websites. The cost of marketing is, well, whatever you wish to spend on whatever activities you've identified while reading this book.

Why do authors using the bargain services buy and sell so few copies on average? It may be because many 'authors' are simply goofing around or producing publications that they have no intention of letting others buy – perhaps they are making a one-time souvenir photo album or printing off two copies of a draft manuscript or thesis. Print cost may also be a factor: the wholesale cost per copy (what the author pays for each copy of his or her own book) through those 'free' services is generally much higher than through the services with higher set-up fees – so the author can't profitably buy copies for resale at a reasonable price.

Why else would the authors buying the more expensive packages buy and sell more copies? I believe that most 'serious' authors really want the extra benefits such as wider publicity and availability, and therefore invest more up-front. With that significant investment ($2,000 to $3,000 for the publishing package and books), the author has some built-in motivation to do some marketing to recover those out-of-pocket expenses.

What marketing efforts are most productive? Although it can be somewhat misleading to keep talking about average authors, I might as well continue now that I'm on a roll ...

Consistent, persistent local marketing can help the average author over time sell those 100+ copies bought from the publishing service, recouping much or all of the initial investment. This means selling at the neighborhood bookstores and to your network of friends and colleagues. It may take a few years, but that stockpile will steadily dwindle. One author told me he would keep sending every one of his relatives another copy as a gift each Christmas until they died or the pile was gone – whichever came first. His book [*They Call Me Fred The Landlord*, ISBN 9781552122327 by Fred Miller] is as funny as he is!

Well, as far as I can tell, the *average* author does very little marketing, and what is done at a distance from the author's own neighborhood has less impact than local publicity and promotions – on average. Of course, you are not average. You are an individual who is full of creativity, as evidenced in the creation of a marvelous book manuscript. If you want to mix together some marketing Ps, and have fun, why not? This may be the only book you ever write – so make the most of the potential for entertainment, education and fun.

When pressed for an elevator-pitch-length summary of the most cost-effective marketing approach, I'll reply, "Start by harvesting the low-hanging fruit. And begin your publicity locally before going farther afield." By this I mean that you will take advantage of the easiest tactics first: selling to your friends and relatives, neighbors and niche audiences. That could launch the word-of-mouth buzz to spread awareness. For your publicity, approach the local media first, then use those press clippings and broadcast interview recordings to impress regional, then national media. And don't forget to urge people to post reviews on Amazon.

I interviewed Patrick Carmichael because I thoroughly enjoyed his first novel, *Inca Moon* [ISBN 9781552128336], about indigenous life in Peru before the arrival of Europeans. It is action-packed historical fiction with a bold young female protagonist, full of archeologically-accurate detail and sex, intrigue, royalty, romance, rivalries, murders, etc.

"I'd a lifelong wish to be a writer," said Patrick, in explaining his **purpose**. "And I'd always wanted to be an archeologist."

After earning a PhD and spending two decades specializing in field research in the Andes, Patrick left academia in '95 (thus forgoing chances for a tenured professor position) to pursue his other passion. He spent five years *unlearning* academic writing and developing a *creative* writing style. For his book, he researched the 16th century Spanish chroniclers, while also studying the publishing business.

Patrick did all the recommended things: trying to pre-sell the book synopsis to publishers, hiring a book doctor who became an agent who tried without success to place the finished manuscript as a book or film project. He self-published "out of impatience and frustration," using an on-demand service. He commissioned cover art, and "went way into debt to market it."

Patrick's marketing mix included glossy posters, sending out 1,400 letters to anthropology departments, historians and libraries – "anyone connected with Peru and the Andes." He hoped this would start some word-of-mouth excitement and expected one in ten to buy a copy – but "I didn't even get 1% response."

There was a splashy press kit for TV and radio producers, including a copy of the book... he got the book into 7 local bookstores but none wanted to refill the initial order... there was some free publicity in alumni newsletters... invitations to do lectures and two readings... yet less than a thousand copies were sold in 5 years of intense promotions. "I put my heart and soul into it."

Nonetheless, Patrick is still game. He's just self-published a great sequel to *Inca Moon* called *Eye of the Condor* [ISBN 9781425100605], while taking on more teaching. For some people, writing – and publishing – becomes a way of life, with a day job paying the rent. And there's nothing wrong with that!

Who knows? Maybe Salma Hayek will someday read *Inca Moon* and star in the movie. There are many now-famous authors whose first two or three books didn't get noticed.

Frank Caldwell is another unrepentant indie publishing addict, with nearly a dozen titles to his credit. His story: "I write because I have to. It's a nasty, expensive habit. Like smoking or alcohol, it's not easy to quit, and like the old saying, if you won the lottery what would you do with the money? I'd keep writing and publishing books until it was all spent.

"There has never been any serious thought about planning at all.

Perhaps that's the reason my books have had very moderate success. I'm my own worst salesman.

"Then, every once in a while I receive a letter, or e-mail, like this, from Jennie Martin, who has the web site www.ifish.net in Oregon: *'Have you ever been afraid to finish a book? To know that when you put it down for the last time, that's it!? Because now it sits on my nightstand, threatening me. It's like the last swallow of hot coffee in your thermos, on* 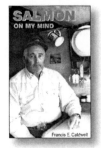 *a cold day on the river. You know it's there, but when to use it up?'* She was reviewing *Salmon On My Mind* [ISBN 9781577854739], my most recent book. One cannot buy publicity like that and it sold several dozen books when she put that on her website.

"Sales are very difficult to predict. Every year we attend the Fisher-Poets Gathering in Astoria, Oregon," adds Frank. "Donna and I decided to write *At Sea* [ISBN 9780966266719], a collection of poems and the stories that inspired them. It's hard bound, has 40 color pictures and was printed offset. We thought the book would sell at the Gathering. It hardly sells there at all, but we probably sell about 1,000 copies a year elsewhere and give some away.

"We've got a website, www.francisdonnacaldwell.com, to sell our stock photos and books. My best success has been word-of-mouth generated by making appearances at libraries and at slide shows.

"My best selling book is *Pacific Troller* [ISBN 9781552122839], first published in '78. Canyon Way Bookstore in Newport, Oregon keeps them beside the cash register. Not because they sell a lot, but because it and *The Prophet* are the most shoplifted of all their titles.

"Right now I'm publishing a trilogy, *The Hawkes Of Smugglers Cove*, through Trafford. I'll market them through the same methods used on the others – promotion trips (visiting bookstores and doing slide shows) in Southeast Alaska, because that seems the base of my fans.

"I enclosed a flyer page in book one, offering books two and three of the trilogy at a discount, plus free shipping. Customers save about $5 per book. To my surprise, as soon as book one was released, 25 people sent me checks for one book that hasn't yet been published and another book that hasn't even been written! Whoopee, can publishing get any better than that?"

A great advantage of setting a budget for expenses in advance is the reality check this provides. Once you look over your available money and time, and review all the advantages you have, some tactics obviously will be unrealistic, while others will emerge as rather obvious to do. You'll then be able to relax and focus on those optimal marketing Ps.

Ray Monigold sold his car to finance the publishing of *Inside the Boom: One Man's Journey Into the 21st Century* [ISBN 1425108067]. It's 30 rollicking stories about a Baby Boomer's experiences living in 40 states, working at more than 100 jobs.

Ray admits to having "great ideas but zero follow-through." As a self-defense measure – against some of his wild nature that is amply described in the book – he and his wife have set a strict marketing budget of $75 per month.

What Ray did bring to the mix was experience and great talent for communicating to large gatherings and through technology: for example, one of those 100 jobs was presenting computer training seminars to the USA's military and largest corporations.

Ray has built an impressive website at www. insidetheboom.com, complete with videos and excerpts, blog (with myspace.com) and podcast. The out-of-pocket cost was minimal; it mostly took time and technical savvy.

He's booking some advertising on popular blogs to sell copies of *Inside the Boom* and drive traffic to his website. "It's very inexpensive – I'm figuring on $50 per month on a 6-month contract."

"You've got to use what you've got," said Ray. "I've got an outgoing personality and no fear, so I'm going to use radio and TV shows – they're desperate for interesting people."

Ray says that financial gain is not his prime motivation for publishing, though he does consider all the adventures he had as his best 'retirement asset' to be turned into a revenue stream and more fun. "My goal is to travel 'round the country giving talks and entertaining."

Self-publishing is definitely in Ray's genes: back in the 1950s, his father paid $12,000 to use a vanity press – a whopping amount when houses cost $10,000. By clever allocation of limited funds and limitless energy and talent, Ray is reaching a far wider audience with a much lower financial investment.

I've talked with thousands of authors, and can assure you that many do become lifelong indie publishing aficionados, just like Patrick and Frank. There are wonderfully rewarding times, and also there will be sobering financial realities. Depending on your temperament, it may be best to make a profit plan in advance, even if this forces you to treat this as a hobby and education you are paying for, rather than a sure-fire investment in future profits.

Then again, if you have a real stubborn personality – like so many authors – you will probably forgo the profit plan and simply *pretend you don't know any better*.... Heck, what's life about if you don't rebel a little at times and take some chances, eh?

CHAPTER 13

Planet

*How will your book's message, its sales and how it is
marketed affect our local and global environment?*

With the release of the UN Intergovernmental Panel on Climate Change's report, public pressure is finally building on governments to act decisively to protect the environment. How forthcoming regulations and people's perceptions will affect the book trade is open to speculation. My own *predictions* are admittedly distorted by my *hopes* for everyone to 'do the right thing.'

Whether you are an indie author, publisher, editor, retailer or other participant in the publishing business, there are many actions that can be done – on an individual basis and with others in the book business – to make a difference to climate change.

The industry norm of preprinting tens of thousands of copies of each book, knowing that about half will be returned and scrapped, cannot continue. Selling books on a 'returnable basis' is a euphemism for 'gross, unconscionable waste.' No one benefits, except printing and shipping companies. Please do what you can to keep your book from being sold on these terms. Only by citizens exerting steady pressure will the book trade change. Please check out my crusade to end the industry's practice of overprinting and selling on a 'returnable' (consignment) basis at: www.BookIndustryBailout.ca.

The paper-making industry is responsible for the harvesting of millions of hectares of forests every year – much of it in old-growth forests and sensitive habitats. It is also one of the world's largest consumers of fresh water – a substance that is increasingly in short supply. Processing consumes huge amounts of power which adds to total greenhouse gas emissions. Paper-making leads to dumping of dioxins and other persistent organic pollutants into the marine environment. These toxins bio-accumulate as they move up the food chain, posing significant health risks to all creatures, including humans.

Organizations such as the Ancient Forest Friendly initiative (www.ancientforestfriendly.com) have already signed up hundreds of US, UK and Canadian book, magazine and newspaper publishers, getting each to pledge to using paper that is more ecologically-friendly. If every author lobbies his or her publisher or printing service to do the same, the movement will quickly spread. Maybe you could send a letter to a mainstream publisher, urging responsible paper selection so you can continue to buy their books!

Print-on-demand is an approach that is less wasteful, and its environmental footprint will be improved as production facilities are added in other countries, so books needn't be shipped so far. Better still are the eBook and downloaded audio book formats – these don't consume resources other than the electricity to excite electrons around the Internet.

Matthew Wayne Selznick, who was mentioned in a previous chapter, published his novel *Brave Men Run* in multiple editions. "The podcast and eBook editions are entirely digital," he says, "so there's very little environmental impact involved with producing and distributing them.

The paperback edition is print-on-demand, so copies are made only when they are sold. That means no wasted paper, ink or other resources."

Matthew's light environmental footprint approach also incorporates benefits for global society – the **People** in our 14 Ps of the marketing mix. "The text of *Brave Men Run: A Novel of the Sovereign Era* [ISBN 141165661X] was released under a Creative Commons Developing Nations 2.0 License," Matthew explains. "This means that anyone in a country designated by the World Bank as a 'developing nation' can make copies and/or derivative works, so long as they distribute and sell those copies and works only in developing nations, and they provide attribution to me.

"I strongly believe in this. If, in some small way, *Brave Men Run* enables an enterprising entrepreneur in a developing nation to raise money or create jobs through the production of, for example, a stage play, television show, film, comic book or other media based on my book, then my creativity has had a tangible, positive effect on the world.

"Also, I am firmly, passionately committed to the DIY ethic and the idea that all creativity is valuable. Many people have found that *Brave Men Run* defies their expectations of what 'self-published' or 'print on demand' means with regard to quality and value. I hope that my example will encourage others to take a similar approach – indeed, I'm pleased to say it's already happening – and will add legitimacy to self-publishing as a whole."

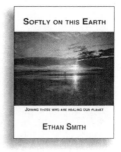

Ethan Smith's anthology of essays, *Softly On This Earth* [ISBN 1412041279] was written to inspire more people to make choices from their hearts, to know that their actions do make a difference and to know that, in their efforts to leave soft footprints, they are never walking alone. He collected essays written by a diverse group of 32 people from around the

USA and Canada. They are environmentalists, artists, musicians, NGO leaders, authors, activists and teachers.

"Self-publishing wasn't my first choice, but conventional publishers weren't willing to take a risk on it because the contributors are largely unknown," Ethan said. "Self-publishing did get it into the hands of many people, effecting more positive change than the alternative – which would have been simply to give up.

"Many people have told me they were very moved by the book. Many have committed to walking more softly on the Earth, treating animals with new respect and a few have even committed to vegetarian or vegan lifestyles. Without any marketing, it has enjoyed moderate sales from as far away as Ireland.

"I have not recouped my investment from this book alone, but it did lead to getting a contract to write another book. So, yes, the results met my expectations. More importantly, it touches the lives of people and affects the world in a positive way."

CHAPTER 14

People

How will your book and its marketing have the most
positive impact – or at least a benign impact – on society
(the local, national and global community)?

W hen I set up the world's first on-demand publishing service,
back in 1995, I honestly didn't anticipate how much benefit
there would be to society. This cost-effective and easily-accessible approach has enabled hundreds of thousands of new authors to present their
thoughts in printed form to the world.

This opportunity for expression and commerce is particularly important for those authors coming from minority groups and lower economic
situations who have been excluded or marginalized by mainstream publishing houses. People in prisons and toiling under oppressive regimes
are getting their messages out. Those who have experienced discrimina-
tion can now have a voice.

Aboriginal groups whose languages are endangered have begun using print-on-demand services to publish some of the very first books in
those native languages. *One Green Tree* [ISBN 1412006260] is a 16-page,

full-color primer intended to teach colors and numbers in Sencoten, the indigenous language of coastal British Columbia's Saanich People. Although this ancient language is now spoken fluently by only a handful of elders, school children are learning it in the local school and it may rebound from near-extinction. The release of *One Green Tree* in 2003 was soon followed by similar primers in other endangered languages, including books by indigenous groups on other continents.

Bothas Marinda of Namibia, Africa, has just completed two books in the Khwedam language of the San people – the famous bushmen of the Kalahari Desert. Despite having no electricity in his village, Bothas uses a Macintosh laptop powered by a solar panel, and uploads pages via a satellite Internet connection.

Why are these indigenous language POD books so important? Because they signal to villagers that books are no longer produced only by white people's publishing companies; now books can be authored by someone from their village. That's a key message for youngsters who want validation, in the face of the overwhelming Anglo-American culture, that their own language is valued and vital. In many cases, these primers are the first books in the indigenous language not created by missionaries (Bible translations) and academics (ethnologies). Ironically it was the colonizers' new technologies that so damaged the native cultures by replacing their communication and reducing their self-esteem; now the most advanced printing and Internet technologies are enabling and empowering first nations people to reclaim their voices.

"A world died when my parents died. I did not want that world to disappear without a trace. I did not want my own life to disappear either," said Sonia Pressman Fuentes in explaining her purpose in writing a memoir.

Sonia's stories about life as a child immigrant to the USA from Berlin,

Germany, and her career as a feminist and legal activist are captured in *Eat First – You Don't Know What They'll Give You, The Adventures of an Immigrant Family and Their Feminist Daughter* [ISBN 9780738806358]. She describes her role in the second wave of the American women's movement, including how she became a founder of NOW (National Organization for Women) with Betty Friedan and others. Sonia was the first woman attorney in the Office of the General Counsel at the Equal Employment Opportunity Commission and traveled the world speaking on women's rights for the US Information Agency.

Sonia retired in 1993 and published her memoir through Xlibris in 1999. She found that "marketing takes at least as much time and effort, and probably more, than the writing. But it's worth the effort. For me, there's no sense in writing if you're not going to be communicating to readers."

Sonia's marketing efforts included giving talks and memoir readings at bookstores, colleges and other venues, and getting excerpts from her memoir published in newspapers and magazines, both in print and online. She identified early on that her niche audience consisted of feminists and Jews.

"Getting the first story published took about a year," she said. "After that, it seemed I could publish articles whenever I had something I wanted to say."

Sonia has received many honors and awards since the release of *Eat First*, including her induction into the Maryland Women's Hall of Fame and the Gallery of Prominent Refugees of the UN High Commissioner for Refugees.

"At first, nothing I tried in retirement worked out," said Sonia. "When I gave up and opened myself up to new experiences, I entered the richest phase of my life."

Many years later, Sonia still has a full speaking schedule and writes freelance articles. Her book was ranked as one of Xlibris's bestsellers. Clearly, Sonia's life and those of her parents have not disappeared; instead they are ever more widely known.

Back in the late 1970s, when oil-producing countries banded together to raise the price for crude oil, a hue-and-cry went up across the United States from vehicle drivers deploring the huge price hikes at the gas pump. That triggered plans for building a massive pipeline from the Alaskan oil fields, through Canada's Yukon Territory, then on to British Columbia and further south to the 'lower 48' states. I was living in the Yukon when construction of this dreaded pipeline seemed inevitable. Why dreaded? The culture of the Yukon seemed fragile – as if preserved in a Northern pioneer time-warp. There were 23,000 residents spread across the territory who would be overrun by up to 60,000 pipeline workers, most from the American South, few of whom would have any idea or appreciation for our way of life or for the environment.

A few of us locals took this as motivation to create a book that would catalog the culture. It would be part ethnological snapshot of a time and  place, and part tourist guide for all those newcomers. If we were successful in capturing in the book what we so loved of the culture, we naïvely figured, the workers would read it, develop a respect for the place and leave it less damaged in their wake. What came to be called *The Lost Whole Moose Catalogue: A Yukon Way of Knowledge* [ISBN 0969007604] would have a ready market of 60,000 pipeline people plus thousands of summer tourists.

Because we had the local culture (**people**) and environment (**planet**) as our clear focus, other components of our marketing mix seemed to fall naturally into place. The pipeline workers were our **public**. We knew the **product** itself had to reflect the Yukon's communal, collaborative social fabric, and therefore decided to include as many contributors' stories and illustrations as possible. This meant rallying volunteers all across the North by the 'moccasin telegraph' and posting business-card-size invitations at every truck stop in the territory. Having about 120 people involved gave us a rich mosaic of Yukon impressions, and also dictated the book's format: a large and somewhat ungainly 11x15-inch, scrap-book-size with small print throughout.

Volunteers did the paste-up and hand-lettered the headlines to keep production costs to a minimum, in keeping with our desire to have the re-tail **price** as affordable as possible. As a self-unemployed hippie living in a log cabin, I had no money, so we borrowed money from my parents and brother (**profit** planning) for the initial printing of 10,000 copies. Yikes!

Place for selling was every bar and café (with **personal sales** by all those authors and illustrators). Every contributor got one free copy as a sample (sales **promotion**).

As legend would have it, we sold the first 10,000 copies within a year and then sold another 10,000. The catalogue remained in print for two decades, and spawned two best-selling sequels, *Another Lost Whole Moose Catalogue* [ISBN 9780969461203] and *Great Northern Lost Moose Catalogue* [ISBN 9781896758022].

Going back to our **purpose**, was this a success? We couldn't claim credit for the pipeline project being canceled – that was a global geo-political decision made by sheiks, Nixon-era politicians, oil lobbyists, the Mafia, CIA, and other characters. We were merely people document-ing the culture we loved, and inspiring others to act in the spirit of that pioneering, respectful lifestyle. Simply through being part of the mag-ical creation of the first catalogue, many of the 120 collaborators felt empowered to pursue careers in photography, filmmaking, writing and publishing.

For example, Max Fraser and a few other contributors formed a local publishing company called Lost Moose Publishing that created the two sequels and published many other fine Northern-themed books.

Another contributor, Jim Montgomery, was inspired to study

journalism at university. After graduation, he became a stringer for Canadian Press working as one of the crew and reporting from aboard Paul Watson's *Sea Shepherd* as it battled with whalers on the high seas.

I personally experienced an enormous thrill from enabling 120 people to participate in self-publishing at its most creative and altruistic level. The memory of that emotional high provided me with encouragement to create on-demand publishing as soon as the technology became available in 1995 and to persevere through the many roadblocks we would encounter. There is great reward in dedicating yourself to working for **people**.

Much has been written lately about a metaphysical *Law of Attraction* that supposedly rewards those with a strong faith and relentless focus on a specific goal. Whatever you envision intensely and frequently will magically materialize is the idea promoted in bestsellers such as *The Secret* [ISBN 9781582701707] and in courses from self-help gurus.

One successful indie author wants to add a cautionary note for other authors. Darla Murray Loomis wrote *Temporary Temples of Beauty: The Sacred and the Marketplace* [ISBN 9781413489644, self-published  through Xlibris]. "If you put your goal out there with focus only on material things (a house or a car, for example) or the financial bottom-line (I'm going to become a millionaire), how do you know what's going to come with it? Are you ready for the drawbacks? What opportunities are you going to miss by being so narrowly focused?"

Darla believes we "need to leave mystery in life. More than attracting material things or obsessing on becoming the best or the biggest, we need to learn to let go. Sometimes you need to get out of your own way and see what shows up. Life gives you lots of messages and opportunities.

"There are deeper realities – if you do what you love, money will follow," she says. "It seems as a society we have forgotten how to do the smallest tasks out of love. We've become so busy trying to make things happen that we don't stop and slow down enough to hear the rhythm of our own living heart."

Darla developed innovative operating philosophies that led to success for her beauty enterprises, and she now counsels companies in how they too can "make transformation your business, transforming each employee's own life and your community." She trains management and staff at organizations as diverse as the YWCA and spa resorts.

In marketing her writings, Darla chose to celebrate creativity and synchronicity. She turned down one publisher's offer for her five manuscripts, to pursue self-publishing instead because "I wanted to have fun with it, and do this at my own pace. I also wasn't willing to change my voice for mass market appeal."

She's had a few signings at Borders and Barnes & Noble stores, each one organized by her husband. "Most artists feel uncomfortable with self-promoting, so having someone else act as publicist feels more professional.

"I'm not going full throttle with promotions," Darla adds. "I'd rather put the book out there and wait to see what shows up, and then follow that. It's like following a golden thread to the creative tapestry of your life. I believe in more organic growth. That doesn't mean I don't plan and create opportunities – I do, but I don't get attached to the outcome. Some simple principles I try to live by are: simply show up – be present, pay attention, always tell the truth, and don't get attached to the outcome because sometimes and actually most the time, you're being led to something even greater than you imagined and more aligned with your true essence."

So what 'showed up' for Darla in only eight months since her book's launch? She's had a surge in bookings as a motivational speaker. Each of those events means more 'back-of-the-room' book sales and opportunities to transform the lives of individuals. And her corporate consulting work has grown significantly, including new work for Calvin Klein.

"I'm helping people see life in a different way, with softer eyes. The business world needs a different grid. Managers need to be open to nurturing, mystery and creativity – it's less stressful than always working to predict and control exact outcomes."

Darla's life and philosophy illustrate how taking the focus off the *financial bottom-line* allows an author to succeed with what she calls the *creative bottom-line* of mystery, life transformation and service of others in society.

Klaus Ollmann, my friend and the translator for this book's German edition, compares life to sitting by a wide river. Instead of running in circles, he sits on the riverbank and observes what's drifting by. New opportunities are coming all the time – some he fishes out if interesting. He is content to throw an opportunity back if it doesn't feel right.

"To help someone who is having trouble – that's wonderful," author Peter Knight of Sechelt, BC, told me. He was explaining his **purpose** for writing and self-publishing *Electrical Code Simplified: Residential Wiring* [ISBN 90920312278].

"Back in the early 1970s, as an electrical inspector, I would constantly come across home-owners who were ill-equipped to do their own  wiring. So I spent countless hours coaching them in how to do it by the Code and safely. They needed help and I was the unfortunate bearer of the bad news that you have to do it over again. So I wrote a book to help people out.

"I didn't have a business plan; the sales end I wasn't too concerned with. If you sit and stew about all the potential problems ahead – you'll give yourself health problems," Peter said.

Back then, self-publishing meant printing copies on a Gestetner spirit duplicator from stencils that were laboriously typed. Peter bought his own duplicator, printed off and collated 1,000 copies in his basement and

took some to a friend who owned an electrical supply store. An unem-
ployed electrician standing nearby spotted an opportunity and asked to
become the book's salesman. He drove around BC, selling 300 copies to
hardware and building supply stores.

Within a month, the first printing was sold out and a second batch
was needed. Still without a plan, as Peter explained, "The next thing we
knew I was in business!"

Because the Gestetner stencils wore out after 1,000 impressions,
Peter's wife had to re-type the entire book for each printing and Peter
had to carefully redraw all the diagrams.

Being a hands-on fellow, Peter soon bought a used offset press, built
his own air-operated guillotine cutter, ordered in two-and-a-half tons of
paper, and kept printing. His children and the neighborhood kids were
recruited for collating and punching holes for the multi-ring binding.
Orders kept flowing in.

After a decade of self-printing, Peter switched to ordering large print
runs from Friesens Printing in Altona, Manitoba. He also agreed to have
a large national book distributor take over most of the store accounts.

So far, Peter has sold a staggering *one million copies* of his self-help
book and its companion technical guide for professionals. What promotions did he do? "I tried some advertising in a renovation magazine at
one point, but it didn't work. Word-of-mouth was the most successful.
When the national distributor came to see me, he said, 'I am told repeatedly that I should contact you.'"

Although Peter didn't have a marketing mix written out, I think he
had his Ps well figured. His **purpose** (helping people) and **public** (those
doing home wiring) were clear. He thoroughly understood electrical
work, the Code and how desperately people needed help, so he created a
product specifically for the untrained person. "The Code itself is a *legal*
document, and even the electricians can't understand it; people needed
something they could easily understand."

Peter instinctively knew the best **place** (hardware and building supply stores, rather than bookstores). He also knew that having a needed product would foster word-of-mouth **publicity** and therefore he didn't waste time and money on **paid advertising** and other **promotions**. The **price** proposition is really about safety and avoiding extra inspection fees – paying $11.95 is a no-brainer for an education and peace-of-mind. Peter's **positioning** is about this being an understandable guide written by an inspector, saving you money and being safe.

Above all, Peter had the **people** aspect of the 14-Ps in mind – society's best interest – when creating this book and marketing it. His book has been used in over a million homes across Canada in a country of only 30 million people. By creating an understandable and thorough guide, Peter Knight likely has had more impact on electrical safety and preventing electrical house fires than anyone else in the country. I think he deserves a special medal from the Queen, and a top spot in the indie author hall of fame.

This final word of advice to other authors from Peter Knight, who has now sold well over a million copies: "There are always problems to overcome and, with the right attitude, you can have a ball solving them. Make sure that each obstacle overcome gives you sheer pleasure. Above all, it's nice to help **people**."

The Book Marketing Mix Template

S ome people might define 'marketing' to encompass only personal selling and advertising. Others might add in publicity. I feel those definitions are too narrow to be useful.

Let's instead view marketing in *very* broad terms. Let's agree to view it as an organized effort that emphasizes juggling a number of factors to place the right product into the hands of the right customers at the right moment at the right price.

There are fourteen of these factors (all conveniently starting with the letter P) that you'll be considering when creating a marketing plan or mix. Before you start feeling overwhelmed, take heart that you've already created much of your book's marketing plan in your head or on paper or in your heart – it just hasn't been written down in the manner of this template.

The questions for each P are at the start of each chapter, and they are repeated on the following pages. These questions are meant to be thought-provoking. Your responses will provide clues to solving the puzzle of what will be your ideal plan. Which factors and tactics would be logical and fun for your book? How much time and money will you devote to each? You may decide to do *nothing* in some areas, which could certainly be wise! A good mix can help you allocate your scarce resources, feel confident and achieve marvelous results.

It is important to get your ideas (especially the lame ones) down on paper – this takes them out of your front-of-mind consciousness and opens up brain space for other ideas to hatch!

Without further ado – here are the definition of marketing and the book marketing mix template questions.

Marketing is the process of **creating, implementing, monitoring and evolving a strategy** for the complete **marketing mix**, which is:

    having a needed **product** (or service)

    available at a convenient **place** (and time)

    for a mutually satisfactory **price** (value),

    while ensuring that the correct segments of the **public**

    are aware (the **promotional mix**)

    and motivated (**positioning**),

    all in a manner which takes advantage of strategic **partnerships**

    and contributes to the overall **purpose** (passion).

The **promotional mix** includes

    personal sales,

    publicity & public relations,

    paid advertising,

    and sales **promotions**.

Ideally, this will be done with respect and consideration to

    financial **profits,**

    the **planet** (our environment)

    and **people** (society).

THE BOOK MARKETING MIX TEMPLATE

PURPOSE/PASSION

What is your overall goal or purpose?

How will you define and measure success?

Can you spell out the goal or goals in terms of personal aspirations, interpersonal relationships, profit, mission or mandate?

What specifically do you stand to gain?

What will you lose by failure to achieve your goal(s)?

PRODUCT OR SERVICE

What product or service will you provide?

What are the tangible results for someone buying and using your book – what are you 'delivering' to the client?

What product development and market research are you doing (such as examining competing products)?

PLACE (DISTRIBUTION & TIMING)

How and where and when will you provide your product?
Consider these options:

- Selling within the book trade

- Hosting a book launch event

- Selling in gift shops and to other retailers

- Trade shows and other large gatherings (industry trade shows, book festivals and salons, non-book-industry events)

- Schools and other educational markets

- Going to the audience

- Selling an eBook edition

- Selling an audio book edition

- 'Special' or corporate sales

What other alternatives have you explored?

PUBLIC(S)

Who 'buys'? Who is your 'target audience'?

What in their behaviors and motivations distinguishes this group?

Does anyone compete with you and might benefit from your lack of success?

PRICE/VALUE

What is the total cost (emotional, time, financial) for customers to buy this product or service?

What is the value a customer gains?

Is there an emotional or financial cost for the customer to *not* buy?

POSITIONING

What makes what you provide, or the way you provide it, unique (i.e., what is the USP = unique sales proposition)?

What is the best concise argument (the key messages) you can make for your product or service?

Assess your identity (how you try to project yourself and your book) and your image (how others actually perceive you) – is there a gap? To be successful, how must you and your product be perceived?

What is your branding? How are you packaging your product/service and your promotions?

PARTNERSHIPS

Who can help in a mutually beneficial (synergistic) relationship? Can you find a way to create a more valuable product offering or package by selling your product in combination with that of a partnering company?

Who shares your selling space without mutual benefit? Can something be done to enlist them in mutually-beneficial marketing?

PROMOTIONAL MIX – PERSONAL SALES

To whom will you be personally communicating and how? What are the key messages?

What specific personal sales ideas will you implement?

PROMOTIONAL MIX – PAID ADVERTISING

To whom will you be communicating through paid ads and in which papers, magazines or other media? What are the key messages?

What specific advertising will you purchase? How will you monitor the results?

PROMOTIONAL MIX – PUBLICITY & PUBLIC RELATIONS

To whom will you be communicating through publicity and how? What are the key messages?

What specific publicity ideas will you implement?

PROMOTIONAL MIX – SALES PROMOTIONS

What will you do as a **sales promotion** for your book?

What are your ideas for **push promotions** to encourage distributors and retailers to stock and sell your book?

How will you bring customers to the retail outlets? (**pull promotions**)

Can your book be used as a **sales promotion** for other products or services?

PROFITS

What are your financial goals and constraints?

Have you prepared a budget?

Is your commitment of money and time sustainable, knowing that a mix will succeed only if you can consistently apply the required resources over time? (Perhaps the fifteenth P could be 'Persistence'!)

PLANET

How will your book's message, its sales and how it is marketed affect our local and global environment?

PEOPLE

How will your book and its marketing have the most positive impact – or at least a benign impact – on society (the local, national and global community)?

PLANNING THE MARKETING MIX FOR SELF-PUBLISHING SUCCESS

At its most basic, your marketing plan can be as simple as answering the questions in the preceding marketing mix template. If you do that, you'll be way ahead of most other self-publishing authors and many industry pros because you'll have a clear perspective and can focus on those factors you've decided to emphasize. As important, you'll have decided, and are comfortable with the decision, on what *not* to do.

May you sell many books and achieve your purpose!

LaVergne, TN USA
29 October 2010
202819LV00004B/15/P

9 781897 435007